SEEDS in SOIL

SEEDS in SOIL

Planting a Garden and Finding Your Roots

 Susan Apps-Bodilly

WISCONSIN HISTORICAL SOCIETY PRESS

Published by the Wisconsin Historical Society Press
Publishers since 1855

The Wisconsin Historical Society helps people connect to the past by collecting, preserving, and sharing stories. Founded in 1846, the Society is one of the nation's finest historical institutions.
Join the Wisconsin Historical Society: wisconsinhistory.org/membership

Printed in the United States of America

Designed by Composure

26 25 24 23 22   1 2 3 4 5

Library of Congress Cataloging-in-Publication Data

Names: Apps-Bodilly, Susan, author.
Title: Seeds in soil : planting a garden and finding your roots / Susan Apps-Bodilly.
Description: Madison : Wisconsin Historical Society Press, [2022] | Includes index. |
    Audience: Ages 9–12 | Audience: Grades 4–6
Identifiers: LCCN 2021046132 (print) | LCCN 2021046133 (ebook) | ISBN 9780870209857
    (paperback) | ISBN 9780870209864 (ebook)
Subjects: LCSH: Gardening—Wisconsin—Juvenile literature. | Gardening—Wisconsin—
    History—Juvenile literature. | Planting (Plant culture)—Juvenile literature.
Classification: LCC SB457 .A67 2022 (print) | LCC SB457 (ebook) | DDC
    635.08309775—dc23/eng/20211020
LC record available at https://lccn.loc.gov/2021046132
LC ebook record available at https://lccn.loc.gov/2021046133

∞ The paper used in this publication meets the minimum requirements of the American National Standard for Information Sciences—Permanence of Paper for Printed Library Materials, ANSI Z39.48–1992.

For Paul, my partner in the garden and in life.

For my family, who taught me to garden
and who continue to help me remember my roots.

CONTENTS

Isn't that a huge pumpkin? That's me between my 2 brothers. Jeff is on the left, and Steve is on the right. We planted pumpkin seeds in the spring, watched the seedlings sprout, the vines grow, and then the blossoms turn into pumpkins. Finally, it was harvest time! We loaded a giant pumpkin into the wheelbarrow.

When I was growing up, my family spent time at our cabin in central Wisconsin. We learned about gardening by planting seeds in soil. We prepared the soil, planted seeds, and pulled weeds in the hot summer sun. When the vegetables became ripe, we harvested them. We ate freshly picked lettuce and tomatoes in salad. I always enjoyed gardening and eating produce from our family garden. I still garden today.

Are you interested in gardening? The first part of this book is called From Seeds to Harvest. It will help you decide what to plant, where to plant it, and what you need to get started. You'll read why gardeners learn about the soil in their region and how to start growing vegetables in a small space or a large space. Once you have a plan for where to plant your garden, you will need some basic tools. A shovel, trowel, gloves, and watering can are handy while you work in the garden. Some seeds are planted directly in the ground at the right time of year. Others are started inside and then moved outside. But what will you grow? Thinking about foods you like helps you decide which seeds to plant. Do you want to grow ingredients for a nice salad or to top a pizza? How about berries? You might like to try planting strawberries, blueberries, or raspberries in your garden.

The next part, Garden Projects, is all about getting creative in the garden. It describes how to find inspiration for being outside in new ways. You'll read ideas for keeping a garden journal, drawing a garden map, writing your thoughts, or sketching things you discover in your garden space. Try a theme garden activity, or plan to invite bees and butterflies while you tend to plants.

The third part is Finding Your Roots. While you work in your garden, think about who raised food on this land in the past. Learn about First Nations gardeners, whose deep connection to the soil shows respect for everything the land provides. Fur traders, lead miners, and people living in lumber camps also worked the land in what would become Wisconsin. They needed food for themselves and their families. Others arrived as enslaved people, immigrants, or refugees. With space and opportunity, these different groups raised vegetables and grains and found ways to preserve food for the winter.

WHY SHOULD I START A GARDEN?

Everyone needs to eat. People like to eat good food. Food grown closer to home is fresh and tastes great! Food picked far away is stored in a distribution center. Then it is transported again to a grocery store. It takes time to reach you, so it is less fresh when it reaches your table. Instead of buying food that traveled from far away, plant your own food, watch it grow, and eat it when it's freshly picked.

You've probably heard that eating fruits and vegetables is healthy for you. Healthy foods can also be delicious, especially when they are fresh out of the garden. As a gardener, you'll have the chance to try new foods after watching them grow. This book has several garden recipes to make with your family.

Gardening is also a great place to dig in and learn about the natural world. Do you know which vegetables grow underground? Which ones grow on a vine? In a garden, you'll learn about plants, animals, insects, and the weather. You'll find out how to make your garden space more inviting to helpful bees and beautiful butterflies. You'll discover what helps your plants to grow and figure out solutions if a problem arises.

Gardening is an enjoyable activity to share with friends and family. You can nurture and celebrate social connections in a family garden, community garden, or school garden. Being responsible for growing things is a meaningful group project. By working together, you can help the garden to grow.

Did you know working in a garden also has wellness benefits? Growing your own food helps you feel self-reliant. Time outdoors helps you feel relaxed. You use all of your senses to experience what is happening around you. Feel the texture and temperature of soil in the ground, hear birds chirping, smell flowers. Observe different shades of color, shapes, and textures in a garden. When you are aware of your surroundings, your body feels peaceful and calm.

Gardening is also fun! Moving around in a garden is a physical, hands-on activity. It's also a chance to experiment and be creative. There are so many kinds of gardens to try. You might even create a new one!

HISTORICAL THINKING

A garden is a good place to think about history. History is not just about events that happened long ago. It can also be about how you understand yourself and how you see the world. Learning about history through the lens of a garden is a way to connect to the past.

What is history? The textbook *Wisconsin: Our State, Our Story* defines *history* as "the study of events of the past and people who lived in the past." Historians are people who study, write, and tell about the past. How do they study history? They use primary and secondary sources and examine evidence to investigate the past. Primary sources contain first-hand accounts, created at the time. These might include an artifact, a map, letters, photographs, or a diary. They serve as an original source of information about a topic. Secondary sources are written by people who didn't experience something directly. If someone does research to write a book or article, that is a secondary source.

WHI IMAGE ID 95703

Rosalie, Ollie Mae, and Adrena Matthews pose near their garden in Madison in 1939.

A seed order form from 1943

In this book, along with learning about gardening, you will practice historical thinking. To be engaged with historical thinking means to ask questions about the source, context, and claims about the past. At the beginning of each chapter, you'll find an image from the past. You'll observe, think, and wonder about each of these images.

When you observe, you identify and notice details. With a primary source, look for details that tell you about who created it, when, and for what purpose.

Next, think about the image, and evaluate the source. Ask yourself questions about when and why the item was created and who it was intended for. Accounts of the past differ depending on the creator's perspective.

Lastly, you will wonder and ask questions. Maybe you've always thought about a topic in one way, but with further research, you might change your point of view. This is when you begin to think critically about the past.

Primary source documents can prompt you to draw from your own experience and then make realizations about what further research is needed. Answering questions about the past takes more than one source. Historical thinking requires research with multiple documents to interpret the past with awareness about which sources provide the best evidence.

The primary source documents in this book are intended as a beginning, to help you understand the importance of thinking about the past. For all topics, you'll want to continue to ask questions, consider other sources, and do more research.

LET'S GARDEN!

What is your reason to learn about gardening and the past? Getting outside in a garden is fun and it gives you an opportunity to connect with other people. With this book, you'll observe, think, and wonder about gardeners from the past and learn how to plant a successful garden today. Plus, eating the fresh fruits and vegetables you harvest is a great way to be healthy and happy. Start planting some seeds in soil!

Two young girls hold up vegetables in their garden in about 1919.

Garden Safety

To keep your garden experience positive and safe, you should follow some basic safety guidelines. Many of these are common sense, but it's a good idea to review them. These suggestions reduce the chance of injuries and illness and help everyone bring in a healthy harvest!

- Wash your hands before and after working in the garden.
- Ask an adult for help with anything difficult. Working alongside someone older is a great way to be introduced to tools and learn in the garden.
- Be knowledgeable of all allergies that may affect gardeners, including allergies to food, plants, sap, and insects.
- Don't eat any plant unless it is approved by an adult.
- Seeds or bulbs may be a choking hazard. Small children should be supervised in a garden.
- Have a first-aid kit nearby.
- An adult should supervise use of scissors, hammers, garden spades, pruners, or any sharp or heavy tools.
- Store all garden fertilizers and chemicals out of reach of children.
- Be knowledgeable about any local hazards, such as wasps, hornets, or snakes.

What should you wear in the garden? For comfort and safety, here's what I recommend:

- Wear garden gloves for digging or handling prickly plants.
- Wear closed-toe shoes or garden boots to protect feet from cuts and stings.
- Wear a hat and sunscreen.
- You may choose to wear insect repellent. Ask an adult for help applying it.
- Sunglasses are great for protecting your eyes.

FROM SEEDS
TO HARVEST

Chapter 1
WISCONSIN REGIONS AND SOIL

OBSERVE: Look at this photo of the 2 boys next to a rock. What do you notice about the size of this rock? Does this photo raise any questions?

THINK: Why did someone take a photograph of this rock? What do you imagine the boys were thinking about when they came upon this rock? The rock was found on the Ice Age Trail. What do you know about the Ice Age? Was the land covered by dirt or by ice during the Ice Age?

WONDER: How is the Ice Age connected to gardening? Isn't all dirt the same? Why do I need to know about soil to plant a garden?

To begin a garden, it is important that you learn about soil. Soil is not the same thing as dirt. Think about it like this: dirt is what you get on your clothes and hands when you are working in the soil. Dirt is out of place and has lost the ability to support life. Soil, on the other hand, is a layer of material forming the surface of the earth. It is what supports plant life. Soil isn't made of just one thing, though. It's a mixture of minerals, water, air, and organic matter. Organic matter is the decayed remains of once-living animals or plants. Fallen leaves, dead plants, and other organic matter break down to become part of the soil. Some of the processes that create soil take hundreds, thousands, even millions of years. When you are digging in your yard, think about how old that soil might be!

There are many reasons why healthy soil is important. Soil provides a habitat for plants, insects, small animals, and other organisms. Soil purifies water, acting as a natural filter as water soaks into and moves through the earth. Lastly, soil processes nutrients, including nitrogen and carbon, so living things can use them over and over again.

Soil is a special natural resource. It is important to take care of your soil to have a healthy vegetable garden. When you learn about the different kinds of soil, you build a better understanding of how to protect it. The soil will be ready for your garden project!

REGIONS OF OUR STATE

There are 5 main regions of Wisconsin soil: the Western Upland (also called the *Driftless Area*); the Eastern Ridges and Lowlands; the Central Plain; the Northern Highland; and the Lake Superior Lowland. A region is an area with features that set it apart from the other areas. The areas do not match the boundaries of the state, such as the county line boundaries. The state is divided into these regions based on the geography of each area and the structures of the underlying rocks.

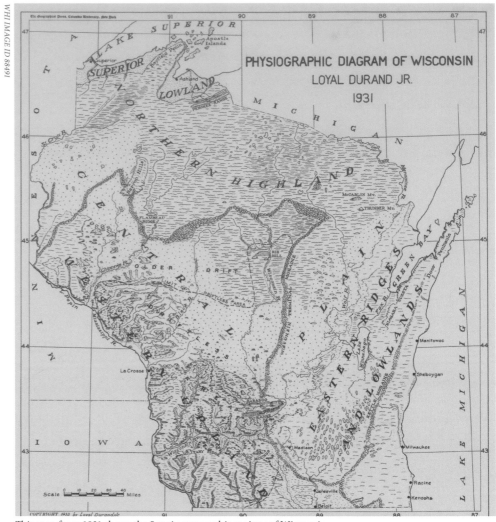

This map from 1931 shows the 5 main geographic regions of Wisconsin.

In our state, glaciers changed the land and created interesting regions. Thousands of years ago, huge sheets of ice spread across the Midwest. They extended from the Arctic to cover much of Wisconsin in an Ice Age that ended about 10,000 years ago. Glaciers carved out Wisconsin's regions. Huge, heavy sheets of ice moved slowly over the land. They were one to two miles thick in some areas. The glacier "flowed" as a result of its enormous weight and gravity.

It did not flow as you think of water flowing from a faucet. Rather, the pressure of all that weight changed the shape of the soft ice and caused it to shift slowly over thousands of years.

As the ice moved, it froze around grains of sand, pebbles, rocks, and boulders. These became carving tools, helping to carve out new landforms. When the last glaciers melted, they left behind all the mineral matter they had been carrying. These pieces became part of the soil. This is how ice movement helped to create the soil in Wisconsin today.

WESTERN UPLAND

The Western Upland, also called the *Driftless Area*, is the area of southwestern Wisconsin. This area was not touched by the glacier of the last Ice Age. Elsewhere, the glacier left behind gravel and boulders, called *drift*, in its path. This area is called *driftless* because there are no remains from the glacier. Because the glacier did not move through this area, the land was not flattened from its weight. That's why the Driftless Area has many rolling hills, steep bluffs, and rocky outcroppings.

EASTERN RIDGES AND LOWLANDS

The Eastern Ridges and Lowlands begin at the "thumb" of our state, the Door Peninsula. This area stretches down the shore of Lake Michigan. This is where you find the lowest point in our state. The slow-moving glacier eroded areas into rivers. It also created kettles, which are formed when part of the glacier breaks off and melts. A hole or pit is left behind. This area is called the *Kettle Moraine*. Some kettles became filled with water, creating lakes; others became wetlands and marshland. When the glacier melted, it left behind soil that was very good for growing vegetation and crops. This region has some of the richest soil in the state.

Wisconsin State Soil

The state legislature named Antigo Silt Loam the official state soil of Wisconsin in 1983. Silt loam was chosen to represent the importance of soil as a natural resource. Antigo Silt Loam is a mix of sand, silt, and clay. The sand and gravel left behind by the glacier is the basis for this soil. The silty top layer, called *silt loam*, is good for holding nutrients and water for plants. The underlying sand and gravel layer allows good drainage. It is named for the city of Antigo in the central part of the state. The city's name comes from an Ojibwe word for the river that flows through the area, meaning "evergreen" or "spring river."

THE CENTRAL PLAIN

The Central Plain is in the center of the state. The glacier also covered this region. It was once the site of an enormous shallow sea called Glacial Lake Wisconsin. An ice dam held back the lake. When the ice dam melted, waters from Glacial Lake Wisconsin carved out tall sculptures, bluffs, and canyons. The meltwaters created deep gorges and rock formations. When the lake dried up, it left behind sandy soil. This part of the state has many stones, rocks, and boulders in the soil.

Farmers pull out the biggest rocks before tilling or planting the soil. In earlier days, before motorized equipment, a farmer might use a "stone boat," or wooden platform pulled by a horse, to help carry heavy rocks from the field. Farmers built fences using the stones along the edge of a field, just to get them out of the way.

In this region, conservationists recommend leaving crops on fields through the winter or planting cover crops to protect the sandy soil from water and wind erosion. Farmers plant trees to protect the soil from wind erosion.

THE NORTHERN HIGHLAND

Long ago, mountains covered the Northern Highland. The glacier sliced off the top of these mountains. As the glacier melted, it left behind rolling hills and valleys. The highest point in the state, Timms Hill, was not flattened by the glacier. It is 1,952 feet above sea level. It is located east of Ogema, Wisconsin.

THE LAKE SUPERIOR LOWLAND

A rock formation on the Wisconsin River

The smallest region in the state is located in the far northwest. It is a coastal plain that slopes down toward Lake Superior. The region is called a *lowland* because it is lower in elevation than the area to the south. The climate is cooler in the northern regions of our state. Woodland and forest cover much of the northern regions of our state.

The Ice Age Trail

The last glacier in Wisconsin was impeded, or redirected by uplands, as it moved south. It split into 6 major lobes as it flowed across the state. When the ice melted at the edges of the lobes, the sand, silt, pebbles, and boulders in it were released. These materials formed ridges or hills called moraines. A terminal moraine consists of the unsorted glacial till at the line of maximum advance of a glacier— the place where the glacier stopped moving. The Ice Age National Scenic Trail follows the path of this terminal moraine in our state. The entire trail—about 1,200 miles long—is in Wisconsin. It was established as a way for people to explore the effects of the glaciation. Most of the path is finished and open for hiking, backpacking, and snowshoeing. The Ice Age Trail Alliance was formed to protect and maintain this special trail.

ALL ABOUT SOIL

Different regions have different kinds of soil. Soils differ because of how, when, and where they were formed. Soil is made of a combination of materials, both living and nonliving. One part of soil is organic matter made up of decaying plants and animals. Another part of soil is made up of rock that has been broken down. Environmental factors such as rainfall, freezing, and thawing act on rocks, causing them to fracture, or break into pieces. Climate, plant and animal life, the geography of the area, and time all influence the rock pieces to make soil.

Soil scientists use a funny-sounding nickname for all the factors that determine soil type: CLORPT. This stands for climate, organisms, relief, parent material, and time:

Climate: the temperature and amount of moisture in the air. These influence how fast rocks and organisms break down, or decompose. Soils develop faster in warm, moist climates.

Organisms: burrowing animals, spreading plant roots, and bacteria. These living things speed up the breakdown of soil particles into smaller ones.

Relief: the shape of the land. This determines how much sunlight reaches the soil, affecting the soil temperature and how much water the soil holds. Deeper soils form at the bottom of a hill. Soil erosion occurs as water moves soil particles and organic matter down the slope.

Parent materials: the ingredients that make up a soil. Each soil inherits traits from the material from which it formed. The original rocks, sand, soil, or clay making up a soil influence its mineral content.

Time: How long have the materials in a soil been breaking down? Soil in parts of Wisconsin is younger than in other places because the materials were deposited by glaciers during the last Ice Age. In the southern United States, there were no glaciers to move materials around, so the soil has stayed in one place for much longer.

CLAY, SAND, AND SILT

Soil is separated into 3 types, based on the size of the particles: clay, sand, and silt. The amount of sand, silt, and clay are what give soil its texture.

Clay is the smallest particle found in soil. Clay is smooth when it is dry but sticky when wet. When it's wet and clumps together, you won't see individual particles. Clay soil can hold nutrients, but it doesn't allow much water or air to pass through. It can be difficult to work with, especially if you are trying to grow vegetables. However, it can be great for flowering plants that need a lot of water.

A Soil Test

Before planting any seeds, do a soil test. A pH tester is a common and inexpensive soil test available at many garden supply stores. This test measures the properties of your soil. The soil pH range is measured on a scale from 1 to 14, with 7 as the neutral mark. Soil below a 7 is considered to be acidic soil. Anything above 7 is considered alkaline soil. Most garden plants grow well in soils having a pH between 6 (slightly acid) and 7.5 (slightly alkaline).

The middle of the range on the pH scale is also best for bacterial growth in soil to promote decomposition. When there is decomposition in the soil, this adds nutrients for garden plants to use. If the pH level is not in this midrange, the plants do not use the soil as effectively. Follow the directions of the test to find out more about your soil. Your local Extension Service or garden center can offer suggestions to improve your soil or help you pick plants that will grow well in the kind of soil you have.

Sand is the largest particle found in soil. If you touch it, it feels rough or gritty. By itself, sand doesn't have many nutrients for plants. Sandy soil is good for providing drainage for plants. If the soil has too much sand, however, water, air, and organic material will move too quickly through it. The plant can't grab these before they pass through.

Silt has smaller particles. The texture of silt is between clay and sand. It feels smooth when it's dry. You might think it feels similar to flour. It also feels smooth when it's wet, but it is not sticky.

Loam is a combination soil with a healthy balance of clay, sand, and silt. Plants need the right amount of each kind of soil to grow. If soil has too much clay, the water may drain too slowly and may drown the plants. Sandy soil can drain water too quickly. But when combined, the clay and silt help retain moisture, and the sand allows for drainage. That's why loam is the "just right" combination of materials for growing plants.

ORGANIC MATTER AND COMPOST

Soil is full of live microorganisms! Every bit of soil contains many different species of bacteria and fungi. These tiny organisms in soil feed on the remains of plants and animals. With this process, they create air space and release nutrients. The roots of a plant need air as much as they need water.

What if your garden spot doesn't have the right kind of soil? If your soil has too much sand or clay, work some compost into the soil. Adding compost is a way to add organic matter and nutrients to your soil. Making sure you have healthy soil is one of the most important parts of planning your garden. Plants in poor soil struggle to grow. Even if your soil is an ideal loamy mix, you should still add compost every year. Soil needs organic matter.

Compost is a mix of decomposed materials. It is nature's way of recycling old plants to help new plants. In a garden, compost helps keep soil moist in a drought and helps drain water if there is too much rain. Plants need food to grow. Their favorite foods are nitrogen and carbon. A compost pile needs carbon, nitrogen, oxygen, water, and time.

You can buy compost from a garden center. Or you can make your own. Your compost pile can be on the ground or in a bin. Choose a flat space for your compost. It should not be located where runoff from the pile or bin drains into your edible plants. It should be protected from pets. You'll want to cover it to discourage animals such as mice or raccoons from visiting.

The best way to start your compost is to stack alternating layers of high-nitrogen items (grass clippings, fruit and vegetable scraps) with high-carbon items (torn-up newspaper, autumn leaves). Begin with a layer of carbon about 3 to 4 inches thick. Then add about 6 inches of high-nitrogen material. Be sure to leave air in between the layers; you don't need to pack it down. Next, add some soil. Then add another layer of carbon and one last layer of nitrogen items. Cover your compost stack with a black plastic sheet. As you collect kitchen scraps, such as fruit and vegetable peelings, you can add them to the compost.

Many families use bins like this one to store kitchen compost until it is ready to be taken outside to a larger compost bin.

Art teacher Sheila Zenk helps a student add water to her school's garden compost bins.

Weekly, have an adult help you turn the pile and mix it up, using a shovel. This gives it air. Add a bit of water if it seems dry. Then wait for your pile to change into compost! It may take 4 weeks to 12 months for your compost pile to break down. You will know when it is ready because it will look darker in color and smell like soil!

When the compost is ready, add an inch of compost to your garden soil and mix it in. Over time, bacteria, fungi, and worms decompose the materials further.

After your garden harvest in the fall, add more compost. Over the winter, worms and beetles will transform the compost into healthy soil for next year's garden. In the meantime, keep adding to your compost bin so you always have some ready.

Some gardeners keep a compost bowl in the kitchen to collect scraps while cooking. Then they carry the scraps out to the compost bin. Some kitchen compost containers have a filter inside the cover to collect the smell. You might want to keep a compost container under the sink and out of the way until it is time to take it outside to a larger bin.

WORMS

Why are worms important in soil? Earthworms create tunnels as they move around. They help increase the amount of oxygen and water in the soil. The tunnels create a natural underground drainage system, so the soil doesn't collect too much water. Worms also eat decaying plant materials that pass through the worm and fertilize the soil. When you find a worm, be respectful. A worm is a helpful creature in your garden!

Composting Ingredients

Nitrogen Layer	Carbon Layer
Fruit peels (bananas, oranges)	Twigs, branches, bark, sawdust
Apple cores	Dry autumn leaves
Vegetable peels (carrots, potatoes)	Hay, straw
Eggshells	Torn-up newspaper
Coffee grounds and filters, tea bags	Cardboard, paper plates, paper bags
Dry grass clippings (do not use clippings treated with herbicides)	

The following things are not recommended for a compost pile because they contain bacteria, attract animals, won't break down, add unhealthy chemicals to your garden, and/or have a strong smell:

Meat, fish, or fish bones	Cat litter, dog or cat feces
Animal fat, bacon grease, or oils	Any plant material treated with chemicals
Milk and other dairy products, eggs	or fertilizer

OBSERVE, THINK, WONDER: Take another look at the image at the beginning of this chapter. Did you determine a reason why the photographer took this picture? If this rock is on the Ice Age Trail, it traveled with a glacier for hundreds of miles. This rock is among many treasures left behind by glaciers.

Glaciers helped to make the soil we use to grow plants. Are you ready to take a look at the soil where you live? What do you think is in your soil? What other questions do you have? What further research do you want to do?

Make a Soil Shaker

A soil shaker is a simple way to observe what kind of soil you have.

1. Find a clear container with a lid, such as an empty soda bottle.

2. Fill the container with water until it is about three-fourths full.

3. Find a safe place to dig up some soil.

4. Add enough soil to the bottle so that is nearly full.

5. Put the lid back on the container, and shake! Watch as the soil floats or sinks. What do you observe?

6. Set the bottle in a dry, cool space. Over the next days, the soil settles into layers. The heavy particles, such as sand and gravel, remain at the bottom, while the lighter ones end up on top. Use a permanent marker to draw a line on the bottle to show where the level of sand is. Then draw a line where you see silt and, finally, any clay.

You could try to make shakers from different places in your garden space. Do the amounts of sand, silt, or clay vary?

These seeds are ready to be covered with soil.

Chapter 2
GARDENING IN SMALL SPACES

WHI IMAGE ID 129807

OBSERVE: What do you think is happening in this photograph? Does it look like an urban garden or a rural setting? What do you notice?

THINK: What does this photograph encourage you to think about? What is this man's opinion about gardening? Can you guess the year this photo was taken? Are there any clues in the photo?

WONDER: Do you wonder why the people are lined up near the garden? What do you think the photographer and the man holding the greens were saying to each other just as the photo was taken? Is this small-space garden important to these people?

A side-yard, small-space vegetable garden

Not everyone has a big yard full of loamy soil. Maybe you just have a balcony or patio. Or maybe you're not quite ready to dig up the grass. And that's okay! You don't need the perfect space to start growing vegetables or flowers. There are several great options for small-space gardening. You can grow plants in containers, or you can build a raised garden bed. These small gardens have other advantages, too. You can start small and add to your garden later. In a small space, you have more control over the conditions so you can create the best garden possible.

RAISED GARDEN BEDS

A raised garden bed is a planting structure built on top of the ground and filled with new soil. Raised garden beds work well for locations where the soil isn't ideal for growing. Perhaps the soil in your yard it is too sandy, rocky, or compacted. If you garden in a raised bed, you'll add soil that is not compacted so the water drains well. With a raised bed, you reach in to tend to the plants. The soil doesn't become compacted from people walking on it. You have more control over the composition of the soil and can plan for the best growing conditions for your seeds. The soil in a raised bed warms up faster than the soil in the ground. This is helpful during a cold spring. Raised beds are easy to maintain and allow gardeners to spend time observing and caring for the plants.

What do you want to grow? Raised garden beds work well for small vegetable crops and flowers. Large vine crops, such as squash and corn, may not have enough room.

Your garden can be any shape or size. The most practical shape is square or rectangular, but you could try something more creative! Most raised beds are between 8 and 12 inches deep. If you are planting over a paved surface, the soil needs to be deeper, up to 24 inches deep. If you build a raised bed over other soil, loosen up the soil underneath the bed with a shovel to give the roots more room to grow. If you plant your garden over a grassy area, remove the grass layer first. Another option is to layer newspapers or pieces of cardboard in the bottom of your raised bed to discourage weeds. Newspaper and cardboard will break down and turn into soil over time.

Gardeners like to be able to reach in to care for plants and remove weeds. To make it easier to do that, the garden should be less than 4 feet wide. You will want to make sure the youngest gardener will be able to reach the middle easily. Some gardens are raised higher so they are accessible from a wheelchair. Older gardeners may prefer a higher raised garden so they don't need to bend down.

Cinder blocks (seen at far right) were used to make this raised bed for a school garden.

There are raised garden kits available, or you can build your own with the help of an adult. The least expensive material to use is wood. Some types of wood work better than others. Cedar boards last up to 15 years because cedar is rot resistant. Pine boards last up to 5 years. Composite lumber is made of a combination of plastic and wood fibers. It lasts up to 50 years but is more expensive than regular wood.

You could also use cinder blocks, wall blocks, stone, or bricks, although they may be more expensive. Stones or bricks could be mortared in place for stability.

My sister-in-law Natasha Kassulke's raised garden beds

CONTAINER GARDENING

Plant seeds in a container and enjoy fresh vegetables in a very small space! With sun and access to water, you can grow vegetables in containers.

If you are a beginner gardener, try gardening in a container to see if you like it. Then commit to digging in the ground later. One advantage of container growing is that you can move your plants inside if the weather is cold or stormy. Another advantage is that you can more easily control the composition of the soil. If you have concerns about the health of the soil in the ground, you might use containers instead.

It's fun to watch your seeds grow into plants with varied colors and shapes. Try growing leafy green lettuces and herbs next to flowers. Or enjoy the bright colors of tomatoes and peppers. Growing vegetables in containers adds beauty to any outdoor space.

These lettuce plants are on wheels, making them easy to move. What creative ideas do you have for container gardens?

PICKING THE RIGHT PLANTS AND CONTAINERS

Tomatoes can be grown in a big container. It should be about 12 to 24 inches across. A 5-gallon bucket is a great size for one tomato plant. Each plant needs to be tied to a stake or placed in a tomato cage to support the plant as it grows.

Both hot and sweet peppers can be grown in containers. Pepper plants need plenty of sun, good drainage, and moist soil. The soil shouldn't be too dry or too wet. Peppers come in all sizes, shapes, colors, and heat levels, from mild to very hot.

An upcycled container garden in Waupaca, Wisconsin

Radishes are another great vegetable for containers. They grow quickly and don't need much space. Other vegetables to try are bush beans, onions, kale, and collard greens. Strawberries can also be grown in containers. You can use ordinary pots or buy a special fountain container designed for strawberry plants. It looks like a fountain with openings in the sides, so the strawberry plants look like they are spilling out.

Once you decide what to plant, start with the right container and soil. Read the seed packet to find out how deep your plant's roots will grow. Your plant needs a container deep enough to let water drain beyond the roots. Larger plants, such as tomatoes, need more room. Plants with shallow roots, such as lettuce, onions, radishes, and herbs, can be planted in smaller containers. The container will also need drainage holes in the bottom so that excess water can drain out. Without drainage, the plant will be too wet. Water builds up and makes the soil soggy, which can lead to root rot. If a plant has root rot, the roots decay, and the plant will not be able to take in water. When your container is ready, fill it with a mixture of potting soil and peat moss or vermiculite. This mixture will help retain the right amount of moisture in your container.

It is important to watch your container plants carefully. Because they are growing in a limited amount of soil, they dry out quickly if the weather is particularly hot. Container plants sometimes benefit from extra feeding with store-purchased fertilizer. Ask an adult for help and follow the directions carefully to use the correct amount for your plants.

UPCYCLING CONTAINERS

You've probably heard of recycling, which means converting waste materials such as glass, plastic, or paper into new materials. *Upcycling* means using something for a new purpose—such as gardening! By repurposing old things, you are helping the environment by keeping usable materials out of the garbage dump.

Anything that holds potting soil can be a container. You could use old pots and pans, an old watering can, buckets, tin cans, and even old shoes. You can repurpose items from the refrigerator, such as a milk carton or plastic butter tub. A colander has built-in drainage holes, and the handles are a good place to add a chain or twine to hang the container. If your container doesn't already have drainage, ask an adult for help poking some holes in the bottom.

Some containers are not safe for growing food and may be a health risk. Plastics that can't be recycled, such as Styrofoam, should not be used for growing food. People do not agree on the use of things like old tires and old furniture for growing food. Before using an upcycled container, research to be sure it is safe for you to use to grow vegetables.

> **OBSERVE, THINK, WONDER:** Remember the photograph at the beginning of this chapter? A newspaper photographer took this photo in 1988. The caption reads, "Milwaukee resident Eddie Patterson holds up a handful of greens he planted at his aunt's home this spring. Patterson was giving them away Friday to anyone who came by. By the end of the day, all his greens, turnips, and spinach were gone. He said he gave them away because people needed the food, and he thought that the drought would make vegetables expensive. Patterson planted the garden about a month ago and vigorously watered and fertilized it. He plans to plant greens again next week and, when they're grown give those away too." In this small urban space, one person grew enough food to share with many people.

Lettuce Salad

Lettuce grows quickly in a container and looks beautiful. Lettuce comes in many colors, shapes, and sizes. Loose-leaf lettuce is great to grow in a small space. Tightly packed heads of lettuce, such as romaine or iceberg lettuce, may grow better in a larger space. Loose-leaf lettuces all taste slightly different, from buttery to slightly bitter or nutty. The texture can be crunchy or delicate. With loose-leaf lettuce, you can cut the leaves right out of the garden. After you give the lettuce a trim, it keeps on growing! You'll see how delicious a salad is when you've grown the lettuce yourself.

In my family, we give the lettuce a trim with clean kitchen scissors. We carry it to the kitchen in a bowl. Then we fill up the kitchen sink with cold water and place all of the lettuce in the sink, immersing it in the water. It floats around and gets clean! Check for any bits of dirt or bugs that traveled in with your lettuce and remove them.

Place a large clean bath towel near the sink. Gather up each clean lettuce leaf and place it on the towel. Then, roll up the towel around all of the lettuce. This absorbs moisture out of the clean leaves. Sometimes we put the whole rolled up towel in the refrigerator. The cold air also helps remove the water from the lettuce. Later, unroll the towel. Gather up the clean lettuce and store in a container. It is ready to eat! It can be stored in the refrigerator for up to 3 days, but it tastes best when you eat it right away. Here's an easy dressing to try:

Vinegar and Oil Dressing

½ cup olive oil

2 tablespoons red wine vinegar

1 tablespoon honey

2 teaspoons Dijon mustard

1 teaspoon dried Italian seasoning or
    dried oregano

½ teaspoon salt

¼ teaspoon pepper

Whisk all of the ingredients together in a bowl until combined. Or add all of the ingredients to a mason jar. Cover the top of the jar with a sealing lid, and tighten with a jar ring. Give it a shake, and it is done!

Chapter 3
GARDEN TOOLS

OBSERVE: What do you think is happening in this photograph? Describe what you see. What people and objects are shown? What is the setting?

THINK: Why and when do you think this photograph was taken? What can you learn from this image?

WONDER: Do you wonder about the tools the children are using? What tools do you need for working in a garden? Why would people like using tools in a garden?

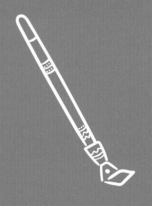

What tools do you recognize in this picture? How do these items make gardening easier?

A boy digs a hole to transplant young seedings into the school garden.

Tending to a garden can be hard work. Historically, people invented tools to make work easier. Using the right tool for a task can make work safer and more efficient. A garden is a place where having the right tool can be very helpful. Here are some common garden tools that are useful to have on hand:

Garden gloves: Gloves for a garden are not the same as winter gloves. They are breathable and water resistant. Gloves keep your hands safe and protect them from blisters or splinters when you work with tools for a long time. Gloves are also good to wear when working with compost. When you're tying up prickly squash leaves or picking scratchy cucumbers, it is helpful to wear gloves. It is also important to wear gloves when you are weeding. Some plants can irritate the skin, causing a reaction or a rash. However, digging in the dirt without gloves is sometimes the best part of gardening! Ask an adult if you're not sure when to wear gloves and when to be more "hands on" in your garden.

Shoes and a hat: In a garden, consider what clothing to wear. Check the weather and plan so you are comfortable. If it's sunny, wear a hat and sunscreen. Unless your purpose is to feel the dirt between your toes, it is a good idea to wear shoes in the garden.

Hand trowel: A hand trowel or hand spade is a small shovel for digging holes or digging up weeds. Use this tool to till the soil, plant, weed, and clean out the garden bed in the fall. The best kind of trowel is light but sturdy with no sharp edges. It has a rounded top. The handle is made of wood, plastic, or metal.

Hand-held garden fork: This tool looks like a rake. It can aerate, or leave air space, in the soil and cut through roots to help you dig up weeds.

Hose/watering can: Watering the garden is an important part of caring for your plants. A watering can is an easy way to give plants the right amount of water. It has a spout with small holes. This makes the stream of water gentle, so your seeds don't wash away or drown. Some gardeners use a hose with a nozzle attachment for different levels of spray. You'll want a hose long enough to reach all of your plants.

Garden scissors: It is helpful to have a pair of scissors just for the garden. Use it to deadhead, or remove dead flowers, to cut twine, and to open seed packets. Wash off the scissors if they have touched any plants that look diseased. Also, don't use dirty scissors for crafts or food preparation.

A bucket is a great place to store your garden tools.

Garden twine: Natural jute twine is helpful in the garden. Use it for tying climbing vines to a trellis or for tying a tomato stem to a tomato cage. It is also useful for setting out straight rows for seedlings.

Garden bucket: A bucket is a great place for your supplies. A bucket is also helpful to collect weeds or move soil. If you collect harvested vegetables in your bucket, be sure it never had any toxic materials in it.

Garden shovel: It is helpful for an adult to use a larger shovel to dig soil or move and stir compost.

Leaf rake: A rake is great for raking leaves in the fall. In a garden, it is helpful for removing old plant material and debris from your garden bed in the spring. A rake is also great for smoothing out soil to get it ready for planting.

TOOLS FROM THE PAST

When you are working in a garden, think about gardeners throughout history. People have always been creative when it comes to figuring out ways to make work easier. The hand tools you use today are probably not too different from tools of the past. The earliest tools were made of animal bone, wood, flint, metal, or tin. Later tools were made of more durable materials such as copper, iron, or steel. Metal tools were heavy to use but long lasting. Some gardeners still use metal tools that are 100 years old or more!

My son Josh Horman uses a row marker in the family garden.

ROW MARKER

Most gardeners like to plant their seeds in a row. This gives the plants room to grow and gives them space so they don't compete with each other. It also gives you space for weeding and walking between the rows. The photo on this page shows my son Josh using a row marker to mark where the rows of plants will go. This marker is very old and has been used by my family for almost 50 years! Instead of marking where one row will be, it marks where 2 rows will be. Josh's great-grandpa built this marker out of scraps of wood. It has 2 two-by-fours spaced 30 inches apart. When it is pulled across the garden, the wood marks the rows in which to plant seeds. Early farmers and gardeners were innovative as they built their own tools to use in a garden.

WHEELBARROW

Did you notice the child in the wheelbarrow at the beginning of the chapter? Would you like to ride in a wheelbarrow? The wheelbarrow in the image looks like it was made of wood. According to garden historian Marcia Carmichael, early settlers in Wisconsin used wheelbarrows to cart around things such as harvested produce from a kitchen garden. She wrote that these early wheelbarrows "could be handcrafted on the farm from reused barrel staves or old plow handles but were commonly factory made." They were also helpful for moving any large load, such as for moving chopped wood for the woodstove.

You may decide to use a wheelbarrow for your garden. A wheelbarrow can transport gear to your garden bed or tote dirt, leaves, rocks, and other materials around your yard. A good wheelbarrow is strong but light enough to maneuver when full.

TOOLS FOR WEEDING

Weeds seem to pop up overnight. When they are not removed from a garden, they can grow out of control quickly, taking over space, water, and nutrition from the soil.

There are a few ways to make weeding easier. First, start with wet soil. If it has just rained, this is a great time to weed because the weeds come out easily. If it hasn't recently rained, water the garden before weeding. It is important to remove the weed all the way down to its roots. If you just break off the stem, the weed grows back. Your garden tools come in handy for digging down to remove the full weed. If the ground is too compacted and you are weeding in dry soil, at least remove the top part, or the head of the weed. If the weed has flowers, remove those to prevent seeds from spreading.

GARDEN HOE

Weeding a garden can be lots of work. You could bend down and pull them out by hand. Most gardeners, though, find that standing up and using a garden hoe is easier on your back. This tool was really important to early gardeners and is still used to weed large garden spaces.

A garden hoe pulls out the weeds and does not disturb your growing plants. It can also be used to dig, mark rows, make a shallow trench to plant seeds, and harvest root crops. Use this tool if you need to loosen up soil or make a hill of soil around crops, such as potatoes. Some have a triangular-shaped metal end, while others have a rectangular end.

ROTOTILLER

If your family decides to plant a larger garden, an adult may find a rototiller useful. A rototiller should not be used by children. A rototiller is a gas- or electric-powered tool. It uses blades, called *tines*, to break up and churn the soil. They come in many sizes and can be pushed or pulled. The most common type is a push rototiller; it is similar in size to a lawn mower. You don't need one to begin gardening. However, if you plant a very large garden, using a rototiller about every 2 weeks helps remove the weeds. The user lightly tills around the plants and between the rows. This also prevents weeds from taking over. Someone still needs to weed within the rows between each vegetable plant.

Weeding is a breeze with the right tools. You might even find it relaxing. When you are weeding a garden, the movement is rhythmic and meditative. It's a good time to daydream, think, or even figure out a problem!

My sister-in-law Natasha Kassulke pulls up weeds with a hoe.

My brother Steve Apps uses a rototiller to prevent weeds in a garden bed.

My brothers Steve and Jeff work in the garden with a rototiller and hoe.

Planting Potatoes

Potatoes are not planted from seeds but are grown from seed potatoes. A seed potato is a potato that has been grown to be replanted to produce a potato crop. To plant potatoes, after the ground has warmed up in the spring, make holes 6 to 8 inches deep along a row in the garden. The holes should be about 12 to 15 inches apart. Use a knife to slice the seed potatoes into smaller pieces, making sure there are one or two eyes, or buds, in each piece. The new plant sprouts from this eye bud. Plant each potato piece with the cut side down and the eye side up. The plant will grow and flower while the potatoes form underground. You might think a potato is a root. However, it is actually an overgrown part of the stem, called a *tuber*. You'll see the roots when you dig up your potatoes. Harvest them about 2 to 3 weeks after the leaves of the plant turn yellow and brown. When you carefully dig under the plant, you will find potatoes! What tools do you think you will need to grow potatoes?

These potato eyes are ready for planting.

Flowering potato plant

Tater Treats

After your potatoes are baked, choose a delicious topping from the ingredients below, or invent your own combination to make it a delicious Tater Treat!

- 2 large baking potatoes
- Nonstick baking spray
- Salt and pepper

Choice of toppings

- Grated parmesan cheese and melted butter
- Cubes of ham and shredded Swiss cheese
- Salsa and sour cream
- Fresh broccoli bits and shredded cheddar cheese
- Bacon bits, lettuce, and tomato slices
- Black beans, shredded cheese, and cilantro

Preheat your oven to 400 degrees. Spray a cookie sheet or large pan with nonstick cooking spray. Wash the potatoes under cool water. Use a knife to cut off any green spots. You can eat the green spots, but they may taste bitter. It is not necessary to peel the potatoes. Cut each potato in half lengthwise and each half into 3 to 4 wedges. Spread the pieces out on the cookie sheet. Sprinkle each potato with a little salt and pepper. Place the cookie sheet into the oven and bake for 20 to 30 minutes or until the potatoes are tender. Remove them from the oven with a hot pad and let cool. Serve with your favorite topping.

Chapter 4
PLANTING SEEDS

OBSERVE: What action is happening in this image? What object is shown?

THINK: Do you recognize the garden tools the man is using? What can you learn from this image? If someone started a garden today, would the scene look like this? What might be different? What would be the same?

WONDER: Do you wonder about the twine and posts he is using? How do you start planting seeds in a garden? Where do seeds come from?

This colorful display of seed packets shows a variety of different plants that could go into a garden. How many root vegetables can you spot? How about herbs and seasonings?

Where do we get seeds to plant in a garden? Plants make seeds that grow into new plants. As a seed sprouts, its roots grow down into the soil so they can take in water. The stem supports the plant and holds up the leaves and blossoms. The stem distributes water and minerals to other parts of the plant. Leaves use energy from light to turn minerals, water, and carbon dioxide from the air into plant food. This process is called *photosynthesis*. Flowers are the part of a plant that produces new seeds.

The seed has all the materials needed to start a new plant. Seeds have 3 parts: the embryo, a supply of nutrients for the embryo, and the seed coat. The new plant, called an *embryo*, is in a dormant state. This embryo is protected by a seed coat while it waits for the right conditions to begin growing. When the seed begins to sprout, this is called *germination*. Most seeds just need moisture and warmth to germinate. When they are exposed to these factors, they begin to sprout.

When the seed coat is broken, the seed grows. The seed coat can be broken by a freezing-and-thawing cycle in soil, extreme heat, or even passing through the digestive system of an animal. In a garden, tucking a seed down in the soil helps the seed get moisture so it can germinate and begin growing. The seed has its own food to begin growing until it produces leaves that will make food for the plant.

SEED PACKETS

Seed packets will provide you with some brief but important information. Take time to read what it says on the back. The planting instructions tell you how deep and how far apart to plant your seeds. You will also find information about when and where to plant them. Do they needs lots of sun, or is some shade okay? Should you start the seeds indoors or put them directly into the ground? It's a good idea to save the seed packets to refer to later. You also can use them to mark your rows in a garden or tape them into your garden journal.

Seed packets will also give you an idea of how long your plants will take to grow. For example, if your seed package says 5 to 10 days to germination, you may see your seeds sprout in as little as 5 days. Sometimes germination takes more or less time than the seed packet suggests. The germination of your seeds might be affected by the soil temperature and amount of light your seeds get. The number of days to maturity is measured from the time a seed is planted to the time you harvest it.

It's a good idea to save seed packets when using seeds.

WHEN TO PLANT

Winter is a good time to begin planning your garden. Decide what you will grow and figure out the best time for planting in your area. Some seeds can be started indoors and then moved outside when the weather is warm enough. Other seeds grow best when they are planted directly in the ground. This is called *direct sowing*. Either way, you will need to do some research into your local weather conditions to find out when you can start planting outdoors.

Seeds to Start Indoors and Outdoors

Some plants grow well when seeds are started indoors and later transplanted, while others grow best when directly sown outdoors. When in doubt, check the seed packet. If it says, "direct sow," that means wait until it is warm enough to plant the seeds outside.

These plants can be started inside: basil, broccoli, cabbage, cauliflower, eggplant, kale, lettuce, okra, onion, parsley, peppers, Swiss chard, and tomato.

These seeds should be planted directly in the garden after the last frost: beans, beets, carrots, corn, cucumber, melon, pumpkin, and squash.

The temperature of the soil is very important for planting seeds or transplanting young seedlings. Figuring out when it will be warm enough to plant is not difficult. First, find out the average date of the last spring frost in your area. Frost dates are the days of the year when it is calculated to be 50 percent likely that the temperature will be below freezing. When the temperature reaches 32 degrees or colder, moisture in the air freezes and becomes frost on the ground. Have you seen what looks like a thin coating of snow on the grass on a cold spring morning but melts quickly? That's a spring frost.

In the spring, gardeners pay attention to the last frost date to know when to plant outside. In the fall, they try to harvest before the first frost date. These dates vary depending on various factors such as the latitude and longitude of where you live, how high the land is above sea level (called *altitude*), and weather patterns. Research the best times to plant for the area where you live. There are websites where you can find out the average last frost date by zip code. You can also contact your local Extension Service or Master Gardener Program for freeze/frost information. It is hard to know the exact date, so it is helpful to assume freezing temperatures are possible 2 weeks before or after the average last frost date. The date 2 weeks after the last spring frost is usually a safe time to plant seeds outside. You can mark that date on your calendar when you are planning. As it gets closer, start watching your local weather forecasts. If your local temperature is predicted to be colder than 32 degrees, you should wait until it is a bit warmer. If the temperature is staying well above freezing, even at night, then it is warm enough to plant outside.

These young tomato plants are growing strong in early summer. As they grow taller, the tomato cages will support them.

STARTING SEEDS INDOORS

Some seeds can be started indoors. The goal is to allow the plants to reach the best size for transplanting outdoors at a time after the risk of frost has passed. In my family, it is a tradition to plant tomato seeds inside sometime after the middle of March. Then, as the plants get bigger and the weather gets warmer in April, the little plants sit outside for a couple of hours. They are brought in again at night so they get used to being outside. Gardeners call this *hardening off*. We watch the plants grow and make sure there is the right amount of water and light. Then we listen to the weather reports. We plant our tomatoes outside 2 weeks after the last spring frost date.

If you are starting seeds indoors, make sure they get lots of sunlight. A south-facing window will usually work best. Some gardeners like to use grow lights instead of relying on spring's changing natural light. A grow light has a special bulb that produces light that is similar to sunlight. Seeds do best with about 12 hours of natural or artificial sunlight per day.

Timing is important for starting seeds indoors. If you start them too early, your plants may get leggy before they can be planted outdoors. This means their stems grow too long as they try to grow toward the sunlight. Leggy plants might be too floppy to support their own weight. They also might not produce as well later in the season.

After you figure out the average last frost date for the area where you live, look at the seed packet of the seeds you have chosen to grow. It will tell you the number of weeks before the average last frost date to start your seeds indoors. Count backward from the frost date to figure out when to start planting. When the time comes, here are the steps you will want to follow:

Bean seedlings growing in a classroom window stretch toward the sun.

1. Choose containers to start your seeds. Natural fiber pots purchased from a store, cardboard egg cartons, and paper pots made from rolled newspaper strips are great for starting seeds. If you use pots made from natural materials, you can put the whole thing in the ground later on. The material will decompose into the soil as your plants grow.

2. Make sure there are drainage holes in the bottom. Set your pots on a tray to catch the water.

3. Fill the pots with seed-starting soil mix from a store. This is a lighter soil and has the right mix of nutrients for young plants.

4. Moisten the soil with a small amount of water. A spray bottle helps make the soil damp but not soggy.

5. Gently press the seeds into the soil in each container. Read the seed packet to see how far down each seed should go. Use a ruler to measure the distance down. Don't press down or compact the soil; keep it loose so that the seed has space.

6. Label your containers so you know what is growing.

7. Place your seeds in a warm location. Ideally, the air temperature should be at least 70 degrees but not warmer than 90 degrees.

8. Some gardeners like to place clear plastic wrap over the seed containers. When they are placed in the sun, you'll create a mini greenhouse over your seeds. This keeps them warm. As your seedlings grow leaves, remove the plastic wrap.

9. Be sure the seedlings don't dry out. Watch the plants and soil carefully to add just the right amount of water.

10. If you put more than one seed in a container, keep the strongest, healthiest looking plants and pull out the others so that there is only one plant in each container.

11. Have fun watching your seeds grow!

Plant Companions

Do tomatoes really love cucumbers? Some gardeners believe certain plants grow better if placed near certain other plants. This is called *companion planting*. This means grouping plants from the same family close to each other. Plants in the same family share physical traits or grow in a similar way. For example, pumpkin, squash, and zucchini are members of the gourd family. They all grow on a vine and need lots of space.

Cucumber plant growing on a trellis

Sometimes companion planting is based on the needs of the plants and how they can help each other. Leafy greens, such as spinach, need lots of nitrogen. Peas and beans add nitrogen to the soil. So if you plant beans in one area of your garden, your soil has more nitrogen in that section. The following year, you could plant spinach in the space where the beans grew. This helps the spinach. When you plant vegetables in a different space from one year to the next, this is called *crop rotation*. Rotating plants in your garden year after year is always a good idea because it helps keep the soil healthy.

Carrot family: carrots, celery, cilantro, dill, parsley

Goosefoot family: beets, chard, spinach

Gourd family: cucumbers, melons, squash, pumpkins

Mustard family: broccoli, cabbage, cauliflower, collards, kale, kohlrabi, radishes, rutabagas, turnips

Onion family: garlic, leek, onion, shallot

Nightshade family: eggplant, peppers, potatoes, tomatoes

Pea family: beans, peas

Sunflower family: endive, lettuce

STARTING SEEDS OUTDOORS

Plants need certain conditions to grow successfully. Picking the right location for your garden is important. Most vegetable plants need about 6 hours of sunlight every day to grow successfully. The garden also needs well-drained soil. You don't want to put your garden in a part of your yard that has a lot of puddles after a rainstorm.

Row markers in a school garden

A healthy garden needs space to grow. Many vegetables are comfortable being near other plants, but some are healthier if they have space to spread out. Read the seed packets to determine how much space plants need to spread out and grow.

Avoid planting a garden in a space where lots of people or animals walk. You will need to be able to reach your plants to care for them and remove weeds. Plan your garden with paths for walking without stepping on the plants.

1. Check the weather: 2 weeks after the last frost, look at the forecast. If the spring air temperature is consistently mild, this helps the seeds. If there is a very hot day or very cold day in the forecast, this may harm the seeds. If a big storm is forecast, then you may want to wait to plant seeds. Heavy rain washes out seeds. A good time to plant is after a rainy day, so the soil is easy to work with and the seeds can absorb the moisture.

2. Prepare the garden bed: Use a rake to loosen up the soil. Break up any clods that might prevent roots from growing. If roots hit compacted soil, they turn away. Seeds germinate and roots grow vigorously in loosened soil. Remove any large stones or clumps. Rake the bed smooth again before you plant.

These pea seeds are ready to be covered with soil.

3. Compost: Use a shovel to mix in some compost to improve the aeration of the soil and add nutrients.

4. Make rows: Use twine to thread across the garden to mark your rows. With a garden shovel or garden hoe, dig a trench for the seeds. Ask an adult for help if the tools are too heavy for you. If you want to be creative, try a differently shaped garden. Figure out a way to mark where your seeds are planted, so you know how to identify which plants are vegetables and which are weeds to pull out.

5. Plant your seeds: Follow the directions on each seed packet. It will tell you how far down into the soil to plant the seed and how much soil is needed to cover each kind of seed.

6. Water your seeds: Use the mist attachment of your hose, or water lightly with a watering can until your plants have small leaves. Keep your tiny seedlings moist.

7. Watch your garden grow!

OBSERVE, THINK, WONDER: You noticed the person at the beginning of this chapter using twine and a garden hoe to prepare his garden for planting. For generations, people tilled soil. Some things have not changed over time. When you plant seeds in a garden, you are following traditions from long ago. Throughout history, plants were transported to new locations as seeds. Immigrants brought seeds from their homeland. That's how many plants that are not native to North America arrived here. Where do you think the plants you like to eat came from? Who ate them in years past?

Hmong Family Gardens

At times in history, people moved to the United States because their home countries were unsafe. They traveled to other countries as refugees. In the 1960s, the United States entered into a war against communist forces in North Vietnam. The Hmong people lived in nearby Laos and helped Americans fight communism in the region. But the US forces did not win the Vietnam War, and afterward it became dangerous for the Hmong people to stay in Laos.

A Hmong flower vendor at the Northside Farmers Market in Madison

Many families escaped by traveling through jungles on foot to Thailand, where they would be safe. They lived in refugee camps waiting for new homes in other parts of the world. Many groups from the United States worked to sponsor families to relocate to Wisconsin. The Hmong families were not able to bring many of their possessions with them. Some brought only a suitcase full of clothes, a favorite musical instrument, and of course, their rich culture and traditions. Some of them also brought seeds.

As author Mai Zong Vue writes, "The Hmong who came to Wisconsin practiced an agrarian lifestyle in Laos. Thus, when Hmong took up farming in Wisconsin, outdoor manual labor and hard work was nothing new to them." Many Hmong families enjoy growing vegetables in Wisconsin today. Some Hmong families garden in a larger space together. They may grow beans, melons, greens, and herbs. Some of the plant varieties in a Hmong garden have no English names. The Hmong refugees brought the seeds from the mountains of Laos. They use the plants to prepare foods that honor their culture. The garden is a place to remember and continue traditions from the past. Many Hmong families work together and sell produce and flowers at farmers markets around the state.

See Yang's Pork Belly and Rib Meat with Collard Greens Stew

This recipe was shared by See Yang, a Hmong American who lives in Madison. See says, "Here is a traditional recipe I grew up eating and loving. Although simple, it is what my people and elders made. Somehow, people in other parts of the world cook a similar dish. Traditionally this is eaten over rice, along with many other side dishes. Don't skip out on adding your own pepper dipping sauce for the meat."

> *1 pound of pork belly*
>
> *½ rack of baby back ribs*
>
> *2 to 3 bunches of collard greens*
>
> *Salt*

Slice the pork belly into pieces 1 inch long and ½ inch thick. Cut the rack of baby back ribs into individual ribs. Ask an adult for help using a knife.

Wash the collard greens. It may seem like a lot, but it shrinks during cooking. Tear the collard greens by hand into smaller pieces, or ask an adult to roughly chop them with a knife.

Fill a pot halfway with water and heat until boiling. Add the meat to the boiling water, and turn the heat down to medium. Add 2 to 3 tablespoons of salt, and let the meat cook for 20 to 30 minutes until the pork is cooked. Add in collard greens the last 5 to 10 minutes of the cooking process. Keep your eye on the pot so it doesn't boil over. Skim any foam off the top and discard.

Turn off heat, and let the dish cool for about 10 minutes. Drain the meat and greens and serve. Enjoy it while it's hot!

Chapter 5
WHAT'S IN THE GARDEN?

Victory Garden
By MARJORIE MACKENZIE

Once our garden was a spot
Where we could rest when it was hot,
While all around, in sunny beds,
Lovely flowers raised their heads.
Then the call went through the land:
Food is needed—lend a hand!

Now, where pansies showed their faces,
Peas are growing in their places.
And where yellow daisies glowed,
Corn is planted, neatly hoed.
In what was once the tulip bed
Chard and lettuce grow instead.

Every day we weed and hoe
And watch the beets and carrots grow;
And every night we kneel and pray
For Victory and for the day
When peace on earth will come and when
All the flowers will bloom again.

Hidden in the picture are two pansies, two tulips, a daisy,
and a carrot.

OBSERVE: This is a poem published in May of 1945 in a magazine called *Children's Activities for Home and School.* What do you notice first? Do you recognize the garden tools and seeds? Do you see the hidden vegetables and flowers in the drawing?

THINK: This is a great poem for thinking about the past. What was happening in the world in the year 1945? Think about the reasons writers write: to entertain, inform, or persuade. Why do you think the poet wrote this poem?

WONDER: Do you wonder about the phrase, "Then the call went through the land: Food is needed—lend a hand!" What questions do you have about this poem? What do you wonder about victory gardens after reading it?

When you're thinking about what to grow, consider what you and your family like to eat. If nobody likes broccoli, don't plant it! And if you really love strawberries, you might want more than one plant. But be realistic about how much your family eats, and be careful not to overplant. If you end up with too much in your harvest, you can share with others. Also consider the amount of care your garden will need. Remember, plants need care throughout the summer. If you are going to be away from your garden, plan for someone to water your plants.

Here are some ideas for what to plant in your first garden:

The leaves of beet plants can be cooked or eaten in salads, similar to spinach.

Beets: This vegetable is a colorful choice. Some people enjoy eating the beet leaves, too.

Broccoli: Broccoli prefers full sun and moist, but not soggy, soil. It looks like a little tree when it grows!

Beans: Beans are easy to grow. Pole beans are great climbers and may reach up to 10 feet tall! They require a trellis or netting for the vines to climb up. Bush beans grow in a "bush" and do not need extra support.

Cabbage: This vegetable can be hard to grow, but it's worth a try. It is fun to watch the cabbage leaves grow. Plus, cabbage is healthful and delicious in slaws and salads.

Carrots: Carrots are fun to grow. Your bright orange garden carrots taste crunchy and sweet. It's a surprise to see what shapes you pull up from under the ground.

Corn: Sweet corn needs full sun and well-drained soil. Plant the corn in a block of at least 4 rows.

Cucumbers: Bush and vine cucumbers thrive when the weather is hot and there is plenty of water. They are sensitive to frost, so do not plant them until at least 2 weeks after the last frost date. Bush cucumbers can be planted in containers and are great for smaller gardens. Vining cucumbers can be trained to climb on a trellis.

Gourds: While you can't eat gourds, they are fun to grow and use in fall decorations. This vine plant produces many different gourds. What grows is always a fun surprise!

Lettuce: Lettuce is easy to grow in a container or in the garden. Lettuce is best when harvested in the spring. When the lettuce is done growing, plant a second crop.

Kale plants are easy to spot because of their large curly leaves.

Squash plants like these are known for growing quickly, spreading throughout the garden.

Melon: Plant melon seeds directly in the ground. They like growing in a sunny, well-drained space. They don't ripen all at the same time, so pick them and eat them as they are ready!

Peas: This vegetable is great to plant in the spring. Green peas adapt to cool weather and tolerate a light frost. In fact, you'll need to plant them early in order to harvest before the hot summer sun. Peas do well in raised beds. Try growing them on a trellis to save space.

Peppers: There are many kinds of peppers, some hot and some sweet. They also come in many colors, shapes, and sizes.

Potatoes: Plant seed potatoes in early spring, when the weather is cool and damp. Try planting red potatoes for an earlier harvest and russet potatoes for harvest in the fall.

Pumpkins: There are many kinds of pumpkins. Pie pumpkins are smaller and sweeter. Larger varieties are good for carving jack-o'lanterns. This vine plant is fun to watch grow and change. You'll need some space for the vining pumpkins to grow. Plant pumpkins on small hills, each about the size of a pitcher's mound, spaced about 5–6 feet apart.

Radishes: Radishes grow so quickly, they can be harvested in 3 weeks! You can plant them in late summer or early fall and still get a harvest.

Tomatoes: Tomatoes are not hard to grow, are incredibly productive, and have so many uses in recipes. You'll need some kind of tomato cage or wooden stakes to support the plants as they get larger. Hot weather and a long growing season are great for growing tomatoes.

Zucchini and other kinds of squash: Squash plants need space to grow. The leaves are huge, and the flowers are beautiful. The squash grow bigger quickly, sometimes seemingly overnight! The plant produces several ripe squash a day during its peak. Have you heard the joke about a person leaving a box of squash on their neighbor's porch and running away? It's because they grew too many zucchinis!

Uninvited critters like this one can damage a garden.

What do you think took some bites out of this cucumber?

WHAT ELSE IS IN YOUR GARDEN?

When you are setting up your garden, it's a good idea to think about a way to keep wild animals out. You'll need to notice what is roaming around in the area where you live. You might look for animal tracks or holes. Animals may leave nibble marks on your plants and vegetables. Sometimes you might also notice animal feces that are left behind.

A tall or wide fence is most effective for keeping deer out. A lower wire fence, about 18 to 24 inches high, keeps out rabbits, but sometimes they still find a way under. In my small-space garden in my yard, I put up one wire fence. Rabbits still ate about half of my climbing pea vines. I added a second fence made of chicken wire, which seemed to keep the rabbits out. I found out the hard way that using one-inch chicken wire is more effective than fencing with larger holes. If you want to keep rabbits, chipmunks, and gophers from digging under, you'll need to bury your fence about 6 inches underground. Wear gloves when cutting and working with any kind of wire. Ask an adult for help with fencing materials.

My son Ben Horman and his grandfather Jerry Apps putting up the electric fence.

Potato bug on a potato plant

Some people choose to build up their gardens into a taller raised garden to deter animals from getting into them.

My family has a garden in a rural area. We have a fence around this large garden to keep the turkeys, deer, and other critters from eating our growing vegetables. It was the tradition of my youngest son to help put up the fence each spring.

Sometimes there are insects in your garden you don't want. They eat the leaves of your vegetables and cause harm to the plants. You can purchase repellents to put on your plants to discourage insects such as aphids, mites, or potato bugs. Keep in mind, pesticides that get rid of bugs you don't want can harm the good ones, too. Minimal use is also a good idea whenever children are near and working in a garden. Sometimes the best way to remove unwanted insects, such as potato bugs, is to walk along the row and pick them off and put them in a container of soapy water.

There are many "good insects" in your garden. These help out by hunting and eating insects that are harmful to the crops. Think of the garden as an insect habitat. The insects get what they need from your garden habitat: food, water, and a place to live. They may be in different life cycle stages: egg, larva, pupa, or adult. Be sure to research insects you see in your garden before deciding whether to remove them.

Planting flowers in your garden is also a great way to attract good insects. Plus, it adds color and beauty. Flowers provide pollen and nectar for the insects. A border of marigolds may help deter rabbits from the garden. Some gardeners believe rabbits don't like the smell.

VICTORY GARDENING

People have gardened for different reasons throughout history. During World War I and World War II, many farm or factory workers joined the army. Some of the meat, wheat, and other foods being produced were needed to feed soldiers. Food became scarcer, so the US government called upon people to grow gardens in their yards. The government printed public information posters to spread the word. The intent was to persuade people to produce vegetables for their own family. The posters encouraged community support and raised awareness for the needs of the soldiers fighting in the war. These gardens were called *victory gardens*. For many people, the food from their own garden helped them have enough food to eat. Many continued gardening in peace time.

WHI IMAGE ID 4762

WHI IMAGE ID 3548

These victory garden posters encouraged Americans to grow their own gardens as a food source during World War I and World War II.

During World War II, food rationing books were issued to each family member. This booklet told how much gasoline, tires, sugar, and other items could be purchased. As during the previous war, people grew their own food in victory gardens as a way to help with the war effort and to supplement their food supply. In fact, planting a garden was considered a patriotic duty.

Today, you may not think of gardening as a patriotic duty. However, many gardeners grow extra vegetables as a way to help their communities. You might already share your extra vegetables with friends or family. If you plan to expand your garden beyond what your family can use, consider finding a food pantry that accepts donations of fresh produce.

Pandemic Gardening

Beginning in 2020, the United States saw an increase in cases of infection by a virus known as *COVID-19*. People began to stay home to prevent the spread of the disease. In many cases, as spring arrived in 2020, people worked from home, and children began online schooling at home. Regular activities such as team sports, large group concerts, and going to a movie theater were not possible. What did people do with the extra time at home? Many people began gardening.

Along with the appeal of being outside and spending time with family, growing food from seeds is less expensive than buying food from a grocery store. This was a help for families experiencing reduced income during the pandemic.

I noticed an increase in people buying all sorts of supplies for gardening as soon as the garden nurseries opened up. Many stores, including outdoor nurseries, required wearing a mask and social distancing to keep everyone safe from this airborne virus. Soil, containers, seeds, tools, flowers, and decorative items quickly sold out. With so much uncertainly, related to a disease people had no control over, people found comfort in planting seeds and watching them grow. They also felt a sense of pride in eating food grown close to home. Gardening became an essential part of feeling normal during a very strange time. Being outside and working with plants became a respite for many during the days of waiting for a safer, virus-free time.

Cucumber Boats

This recipe is easy and tastes like summer! Eat the salad and the boat.
To make this recipe, I first cut off the part nibbled by a chipmunk. I can see the little nibbles and know where to cut. Some gardens end up with so many cucumbers that you have extra to share with others. Think about ways to help others with your garden!

- 6 cucumbers, 3 that are large enough to be the "boats"
- ½ cup sour cream
- 3 tablespoons mayonnaise
- 1 tablespoon white or tarragon vinegar
- 1 teaspoon sugar
- 1 large or 2 small tomatoes
- 2 to 3 teaspoons dried dill or cilantro

Wash and dry off all of the cucumbers. Cut the 3 larger cucumbers in half lengthwise; you will have 6 pieces. Scoop out the seeds to make a "boat." If it won't sit up, use a potato peeler to peel off a bit of the bottom to make a flatter edge. Set these aside.

If you don't want to eat the cucumber seeds, use a spoon to remove them. Carefully slice the remaining cucumbers into bite-sized pieces. Put the pieces into a bowl.

In another bowl, combine the sour cream, mayonnaise, vinegar, and sugar. Mix them up. Add this dressing to the bowl with the bite-sized cucumbers, and stir to cover all of the pieces.

With a spoon, fill each "boat" with some cucumber salad. Top the boat with tomato and the dried dill or cilantro.

Emergency Poster 5   May, 1917

AN ACRE OF ROOTS
Will Winter Your Stock

Sow root crops in the new clearing or among the stumps. Every settler can grow roots, while many would not have land suitable for corn.

An acre of roots will help feed 10 cows next winter. Feed will be high; roots will help the settler keep more cows and make more money.

Why Grow Roots?

1. **Big Yields**
 —300 to 500 bushels an acre an average

2. **Do Well on New Lands**
 —Sow them broadcast Weeds won't bother

3. **Low Seed Cost**
 —40c to $1.25 a pound
 —$1.50 to $6.00 an acre

4. **Easy to Grow**
 —Requires no expensive tools

5. **Upper Wisconsin Climate Ideal for Crop**
 —Cool nights helpful
 —Plenty of moisture present

6. **Feeds Man and Beast**
 —Many sold potatoes last winter for fancy prices and ate rutabagas

Big Roots Cut Feed Bills

Nature's silos, packed with food for the settler's stock, the first winter.

Millions of hungry folk next fall will want your milk and meat.

The State Council of Defense wants you to produce them.

Why Feed Roots?

1. **Relished by All Stock**

2. **Keep Animals Healthy**
 —Good tonic
 —As digestible as grain

3. **Provide Winter Succulence**
 —Take place of silo the settler's first winter

4. **Roots as Good as Grain**
 Pound for pound with water out
 —Roots will cut by one-half grain feed without reducing milk yield
 —Feed cows 25 to 50 pounds a day, depending on taste

5. **Keep Breeding Stock in Prime Condition**

Preparing and Cultivating the Soil

Preparing Soil
Double-disk in spring.

Harrow well to produce fine seed bed. If you have it, apply stable manure liberally before last harrowing.

New soil needs practically no cultivating after seeding.

Old Soil
Begin tillage early to get ahead of weeds. Cultivate regularly to keep dust mulch. Continue cultivation until leaves shade the ground.

Don't be afraid to use the hoe.

RUTABAGAS	TURNIPS	MANGELS	CARROTS
Sow broadcast or plant in rows 18-24 inches apart, ½-inch deep. Thin to 8-12 inches when plants have 4 leaves. Plant about June 10-15 in upper Wisconsin, June 25, July 1 in southern part. Use 4 to 5 pounds of seed an acre. When broadcasted 5 to 6 pounds. Varieties:— Purple Top Swede, Golden Neckless.	Broadcast on new soil free from weeds. Mix seed, if you can, with coarse sand half and half to prevent overseeding when broadcasting. When planted in rows sow 24-30 inches apart, ½-inch deep. Seed about June 20, July 10. Use 2 pounds an acre. Varieties:— Early: White Egg, Early Milen Late: Purple Top White Globe.	Plant only in rows 24 inches apart, 1-inch deep. Thin to 8 inches. Seed as early as you can get the ground ready; if possible before June 1. Use 8 pounds an acre. Varieties:— Golden Tankard Long Red.	Plant only in rows 20-24 inches apart, ½-inch deep. Thin to 4 inches. Seed as early as the ground is fit; preferably before June 1. Use 4 pounds an acre. Varieties:— for heavy soils: Ox Heart. for average soils: Chantenay or Danvers. for stock food: Improved Short White.

More cows and more roots will make you money while you are clearing your farm.

Why not buy one or two more cows? Roots will help you feed them over the winter.

Prepared under the direction of the State Council of Defense by the
Agricultural Experiment Station, The University of Wisconsin
Madison

Next fall write for folder on storing and feeding root crops

"More Food This Year Is Patriotism"

OBSERVE: This is a poster featuring a large root vegetable. Do you notice the many statements encouraging a farmer or gardener to plant vegetables, such as turnips or rutabagas? Can you guess what this phrase might mean: "Sow root crops in the clearing or among the stumps"?

THINK: Practice historical thinking with this poster. The small print reads, "Emergency poster 5, May, 1917." What do you know about world events in 1918? What was the purpose for producing this poster? Who do you think was the audience?

WONDER: Do you wonder why there was an emphasis on planting root crops? What other questions do you have about this poster?

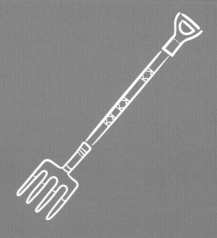

A rutabaga is a root that we eat.

Broccoli is a flower that we eat.

When your garden starts growing, it is great fun to watch all the parts of
the plant as they appear. When you grow root vegetables, you see the leaves.
However, you won't see the vegetable until harvest. On other plants, you can
watch the vegetable as it grows larger or changes color. What parts of the plant do
we eat? How does each part help the plant? The basic parts of most plants are:

Seed: The seed is like a suitcase. It contains the beginnings of a young plant
and stored food. When conditions are right, it grows.

Root: The roots grow down into the soil and anchor the plant. They take
in water and nutrients from the soil for the plant. Some plants have fibrous
roots with many branches that grow from the stem. Other plants have a
thick taproot. A taproot is a large, central root from which other smaller
roots sprout. Carrots and beets are taproots we eat. Taproots store food and
water for the plant.

Stem: The stem supports the leaves. Water, food, and nutrients move up through the stem. A tree trunk is the stem for the tree. A sunflower has a tall stem supporting the flower. Celery is an example of a stem that we eat.

Leaf: This part of the plant makes the food for the plant. The process is called *photosynthesis*. Photosynthesis is when plants use sunlight, water, and carbon dioxide to create their own food and grow. Plants release excess oxygen into the air.

Flower: The flower is the part of the plant that is responsible for making new seeds.

Fruit: A fruit is the fleshy substance that surrounds the seed of a flowering plant. It is called a *fruit* if there are seeds inside. Tomatoes, cucumbers, and pumpkins are the "fruit" of the plant.

Signs in English and Spanish explain the seeds, leaves, and fruits that we eat.

Plant Parts Salad

For this salad, try to include different plant parts. Wash each fruit or vegetable in cold water and dry thoroughly. Carefully cut them into bite-sized pieces. Toss all ingredients in a bowl and then put them into individual dishes. Top with salad dressing. Choose ingredients from the list below, or find your own. Then enjoy your plant parts salad!

Root: *carrot, beet, radish, turnip*

Stem: *asparagus, celery, rhubarb*

Leaves: *cabbage, greens, kale, lettuce, romaine, spinach, Swiss chard*

Seeds: *bean, corn, pea, pumpkin seed, sunflower seed*

Flower: *broccoli, cauliflower*

Fruit: *cucumber, melon, pepper, strawberry, tomato*

Cabbage plant

HELPING PLANTS GROW

As you garden, you learn that plants, like all living things, have basic needs: water, nutrition, space, air, light, and the right temperature to grow. You will need to tend to your plants' needs throughout the growing season to keep them healthy until harvest time.

WATER

Be sure your plants have a safe water source. Water provided by your utility company is generally a safe source. If your garden water comes from a private well, pond, or river, test regularly to be sure it is clean. Some families also collect water in a rain barrel. Rainwater flows through a gutter into a large container so that it can be used for watering. The barrel will usually have a faucet where you can fill a watering can or connect a hose. Water collected in a rain barrel is not potable, or safe, for people to drink without treating it first.

Paul and Joel Bodilly, Pat and Tyler Albersman, and Jeff and Libby Apps check to see what's growing in the family garden.

Watering isn't hard, but it's not something to skip while your plants are growing. Your garden's watering needs will change depending on the weather. Watering on a schedule, such as choosing to water every Tuesday morning, may not work. Instead, watch the weather, and keep track of rain in the forecast and the amount of rain your plants get. Making or purchasing a rain gauge helps with this. A rain gauge is an instrument used to gather and measure the amount of liquid precipitation, or rain, in an area. After a rainfall, it is fun to check the rain gauge to see how many inches it rained. Empty the rain gauge so it is ready for the next rainfall. A good rule of thumb for plants in vegetable gardens is one inch of water per week. (Plants in containers need more than this.) You can also check the soil in your garden to see if it needs more water. Plants need moisture at least an inch or two below the surface to get water to the roots. Poke a finger into the soil to check this. If the soil is dry just below the surface, your plants could probably use some more water.

Too much water can also be a problem for a garden, so don't get carried away. If it hasn't rained, a slow mist from a hose or a sprinkler is better for the plants than dumping large amounts of water on them all at once. Watering slowly prevents water from puddling and washing away the soil. The water needs to soak in. Some gardeners like to use a soaker hose. This kind of hose has holes throughout the length of the hose and provides a fine mist of water.

Water your garden in the morning or at night. If you water in the middle of the day, lots of water will evaporate. Remember, wind also dries out plants. Try to water your garden when it's not too windy so that the water doesn't blow away from your plants. You'll know if your garden plants are happy and healthy by observing them. If the leaves look dry and wilted, they are telling you something; your plants need more water. If the soil remains too wet and is not soaking in, you overwatered. You'll become an expert as you observe and take care of the soil conditions while your plants grow.

FOOD FOR YOUR PLANTS

Didn't we say plants get what they need from nutrients in the soil? The answer is yes, plants do get what they need from the soil and air. However, if plants grow in the same place year after year, they may use up most of the nutrients in the soil. That's why it is important to compost and care for your garden soil. However, adding compost sometimes isn't enough to replace nutrients depleted from growing plants in the same space. Sometimes other factors, such as erosion or wind, also change the soil.

If your family chooses to add fertilizer to the soil in a garden, do this in the spring. Fertilizing is a balancing act. Too much fertilizer is bad for the plants. It will not help you grow giant plants. Likewise, too little nutrition in the soil will not grow healthy plants. It's a good idea to use a store-purchased soil test in the spring to determine how much nitrogen is in your soil before applying any fertilizer. It's very simple to use, and you'll be less likely to overfertilize. Plants need a mix of nitrogen, phosphorus, and potassium.

Nitrogen is responsible for the growth of leaves on a plant. Without enough nitrogen, the plant leaves may turn yellow. With too much, your plants might grow big and green, but they may not produce any flowers or fruit. Phosphorus is responsible for root growth. It also is needed for flowers to develop and bloom.

Potassium is a nutrient that helps the overall function of the plant and helps it resist disease. The right amount of potassium also affects the quality of fruit. If your plants don't have enough, you may notice fruits are thin-skinned or small.

When you understand the ingredients in chemical fertilizer, this helps you determine which kind to buy. The fertilizer bag has letters on it, N-P-K, which stand for *nitrogen*, *phosphorus*, and *potassium*. General-purpose fertilizers have numbers on the bag, such as 20-20-20. This means there is the same amount of each chemical in the bag. Purchase fertilizer with lesser or greater amounts of each depending on your needs. There are water-soluble, granule, and concentrated liquid fertilizers. The water-soluble mix must be applied and mixed with water. The granule mix releases nutrients slowly and lasts longer.

In a raised bed like this one, you can make your own soil mix. Adding lots of compost to your garden soil will provide your plants with the food they need.

Some gardeners prefer not to add nutrients to the soil with chemicals. They plant an organic garden. *Organic* means related to or coming from living matter. Organic gardeners use only compost and natural materials to add nutrients to the soil. Organic fertilizers are also available. Common organic fertilizers are made from manure. Manure is a good source of nitrogen. It is not recommended to use cat or dog manure in a garden or compost bin. Horse, cow, and chicken manures are the most commonly used as fertilizer. Other organic fertilizer may be made from blood meal, bone meal, or liquid seaweed.

You should plan to fertilize outside in the spring, when plants are getting ready to grow. Try to apply fertilizer before a rainfall; the rain helps it to soak in. Do not apply it on a rainy or windy day; it will wash or blow away. You don't need to fertilize your indoor seedlings. However, plants in containers or in the garden bed may need some extra nutrition.

Fertilizer can be hazardous to people and pets, so use it safely. Be sure to follow the package directions, wear gloves, and work with an adult. It's never a good idea to leave fertilizer open and available to kids or pets. Be sure to store fertilizer in a locked cupboard or shed.

OBSERVE, THINK, WONDER: The poster at the beginning of this chapter was a promotion for Wisconsin settlers in the northern part of the state. The poster was prepared under the direction of the "State Council of Defense by the Agricultural Experiment Station, the University of Wisconsin–Madison." In 1917, when the poster was made, the United States was in the middle of World War I. US participation in this war lasted from April 1917 to the war's end on November 11, 1918. The poster describes the notion that planting an acre of root vegetables helps feed cows over the winter. It also describes growing food as patriotic.

The Settlement Cook Book

Elizabeth "Lizzie" Black was born in 1858. Her parents were from Jewish families from England and Bavaria, which is now part of Germany. She grew up and married Simon Kander. Lizzie Kander was interested in helping immigrant families. In 1900, she combined her Jewish Mission group with another organization to form a settlement house. Settlement houses provided services to newly arrived immigrants. Mrs. Kander was elected president. Along with her duties, she taught cooking classes. The purpose of the classes was to teach nutrition as well as methods of preparing food. To help with funding, Lizzie Kander wrote and published a cookbook. The recipes are a mixture of German, Eastern European, Jewish, and American cooking. The book contains more than recipes. Chapter 1 of the book includes "Household Rules." This section has instructions for how to measure ingredients, definitions of cooking terms, and information about nutrition. There are directions for how to "lay the table," or set the table. The cookbook also describes how to wash dishes, sweep a room, remove stains from clothing, and air out a room. Lizzie's cookbook was very large! To pay for the publishing of the book, she sold advertisements printed in the back of the book. The cookbook doesn't mention growing a garden. However, the emphasis on using fresh vegetables and fruits implies that a kitchen garden helped inspire Lizzie to create these recipes. In the recipe on the next page, 1 pint equals about 2 cups each of peas and carrots.

Pages from *The Settlement Cook Book*

Carrots and Peas, from *The Settlement Cookbook*

1 pint carrots

1 pint peas, cooked

2 tablespoons flour

2 tablespoons butter

½ cup soup stock

½ cup carrot water

Wash, scrape, and cut carrots into small cubes. Cook in some water until tender; drain and reserve ½ cup carrot water. Mix carrots well with cooked peas. Sprinkle with flour, salt, sugar, and pepper to taste. Add butter, soup stock, and carrot water. Boil a little longer and serve.

Peas growing on a vine

Fresh carrots from the Apps family garden

Chapter 7
FRUIT IN THE GARDEN

OBSERVE: What do you see in this photograph? What do you notice that might give you clues about when this photo was taken?

THINK: This photograph was taken by Arthur Vinje. Mr. Vinje was a photographer for the *Wisconsin State Journal* from 1914 to 1962. Why do you think this photo appeared in a newspaper? Would you expect to see a photograph like this in a newspaper or in an online publication today?

WONDER: What do you wonder about? What are they going to do with all of those strawberries? Is fruit something to grow in a garden?

Can you grow fruit in a garden? The answer is yes! Some people try growing fruit trees, such as apple, pear, or plum. Gardeners can grow berries in a garden. Raspberries, blueberries, and strawberries are great fruits to try growing.

HARDINESS ZONES

When you begin a garden, it is important to learn about the hardiness zone where you live. What is a hardiness zone? The US Department of Agriculture's Plant Hardiness Zone Map helps gardeners determine if a plant is likely to grow and survive at a location. Some plants can survive in extreme cold. Others grow best in places with a warmer winter. The zones on the map are based on the average lowest temperature each area experiences during winter. Different parts of Wisconsin are in hardiness zones 2, 3, 4, and 5. In the farthest north part of Wisconsin, the coldest winter temperatures average between −45 and −40 degrees Fahrenheit. This region is in zone 2. In the southern part of Wisconsin, the coldest winter temperatures average between −15 and −10 degrees Fahrenheit. This part of the state is in zone 5. Research to determine the hardiness zone for the area where you live.

Fruit plants are perennial plants. This means you leave them in the garden over the winter and it will grow again the next year. Perennials need to survive the cold winter temperatures to produce fruit every year. This is why it is important to pay attention to the hardiness zone of your area.

Annual and Perennial Plants

What is the difference between an annual and a perennial? An annual is a plant that lives through one growing season. When you plant a perennial, it regrows for 2 or more years. Some fruits and vegetables, including berries, rhubarb, and asparagus, come from perennial plants. But some perennial plants will survive the winter only in certain temperatures. Check your hardiness zone to determine if a perennial plant will be successful in your area.

Raspberries are ready to be picked when they are brightly colored and easily detach from the stem.

The Bodilly family raspberry patch

RED RASPBERRIES

Raspberries are sweet and delicious. Summer-bearing raspberries grow on canes, which look like sticks. It's hard to believe such great tasting berries grow from a "stick"! New shoots come up in the spring. These new canes will not produce fruit in their first year. They only have leaves. The next summer, they produce flowers and then fruit.

When you order raspberry plants from a catalog, choose ones that grow well in your hardiness zone. You will receive dormant, bare-root plants. If the roots seem dry when you get them, soak them in a bucket of water for one hour. Then, plant the raspberry plant in a hole twice as wide and twice as deep as the bare roots.

Raspberries spread and send up new canes every year. It's a good idea to plan space just for raspberries; don't plant them in the middle of your vegetable garden. The rows should allow space for the plants to spread out. The new canes will not pay attention to your rows; raspberries spread a little more each year.

In our family raspberry patch, we don't keep our plants in rows. They tend to come up and grow wherever they want! If you'd like a more orderly patch, you can pull out or move the canes so your rows stay neat.

Some varieties grow very tall and may require a trellis or other support to climb on. Gardeners use all kinds of things to stake up their plants, even an old hockey stick! A common support system is to install a tall post at either end of the row and string wires between the 2 posts. You can train the plants to grow up between the wires to keep them from falling over. Installing a post-and-wire system supporting the canes also makes the berries easier to pick. The plants are a bit scratchy. Planning a pathway for berry pickers to move among the plants is a good idea. You should continually harvest berries during the peak season. The plant keeps producing more fruit.

Trim out old raspberry canes in the winter when the leaves have stopped sending energy down to the roots. You will know they are old when they turn brown. Also, thin out the weaker, smaller canes. In the spring, before new growth starts, thin out the remaining small canes and leave the strongest and largest canes to grow.

If rabbits live in your area, it is a good idea to fence off your raspberry patch for the winter. Otherwise, hungry rabbits may eat the raspberry canes right down to the snow.

BLUEBERRIES

Blueberries are an easy fruit to grow. The plant has pretty spring flowers, summer fruit, and beautiful fall foliage. You should purchase blueberry plants that will grow well in your hardiness zone. You will also need to be sure your soil is acidic. You can use the soil test on page 16 to find out. Blueberries thrive in soil with a pH of 5 or less. Blueberries don't grow well in heavy, clay soil. Planting blueberries in a raised bed or in a large container is a good idea if the soil in your region is not good for blueberries. If you plant them in a container, be sure it has holes for drainage in the bottom.

Blueberries prefer full sun. Do not plant them near trees, as the tree roots take moisture in the soil away from the blueberries. The roots of the blueberry are shallow. This means they will need to be watered frequently. The soil should also drain well, though, so they don't sit in too much water.

Purchase blueberry plants as bare-root plants or buy well-rooted transplants. To plant them, dig holes twice as wide and twice as deep as the roots of the plant. Most likely, the hole will be about 20 inches wide and 20 inches deep. Set the bush in the hole with the roots spread out. Fill the hole with dirt. Space blueberry bushes apart in rows. They do best with about 2 to 4 inches of mulch over the roots to prevent weeds and help to retain moisture in the roots. Mulch is a layer of material placed over the soil. In a vegetable garden, dry leaves, grass clippings, straw, or seedless hay can be used as mulch. If you use grass clippings, be sure to use clippings that are free from chemicals.

You may want to let your new plant fully grow and develop for the first one or two years without producing any fruit. To do this, pinch off the blossoms when they grow. This way the plant's growth will be focused on its root system instead of producing fruit.

By the second or the third year, your blueberry plants will be strong and ready to produce a good crop. Watch the blossoms grow into berries. Blueberries are ready to pick when they fall off right into your hand. When they turn blue, you should wait for about 2 more days for the berry to be fully ripe.

For the first few years, it is not necessary to do any pruning on your blueberry plants. Pruning means to cut away dead or overgrown branches to increase the growth of the rest of the plant. After the fourth year, cut out dead, broken, or weak shoots. With larger bush varieties, prune off wood that is drooping to the ground or crowding out the center of the bush. Pruned plants do not bear fruit the following season, so prune a different portion of your patch each year.

STRAWBERRIES

If you love strawberries, should you attempt to grow your own? Absolutely! The taste of strawberries picked from your own garden is outstanding. When they are red and ready to pick, you'll be picking them every 2 to 3 days. With a light twist, the berry pulls away from the plant. Wash and eat it!

One kind of strawberry plant is called *June-bearing*. These berries produce one crop of sweet, juicy berries from spring to early summer. A second kind of berries is called *everbearing*. These plants produce berries in June, followed by lighter crops through the rest of the summer until the first frost. While the name sounds like they produce berries constantly, there are actually gaps of time between crops. If you live in hardiness zone 5 or colder, you may need to replace your everbearing plants every one to two years.

A popular kind of strawberry is day-neutral. These strawberries produce a larger harvest of berries in June followed by lighter crops throughout the summer. Depending on the weather, they may produce fruit for most of the summer. Their name comes from the fact that they begin making fruit regardless of the length of daylight. This variety of strawberry is an annual. It will grow for one season and need to be replaced with new plants the following year.

Young strawberry plants early in the season

Strawberries from a large pick-your-own patch

You can purchase strawberry seeds or seedlings to plant. If you buy seeds, you'll germinate them inside and transplant the seedlings outside once they sprout. It is easier to purchase seedling plants. If you order strawberry plants from a seed catalog, you will receive bare-root, dormant plants. Plant these early in spring as soon as the last frost has past. You can also buy strawberry plants from garden centers.

Strawberry plants like space away from other plants and trees. Many gardeners choose a raised garden, special flower pot, or other space just for strawberries. To plant strawberries, place them in the ground 12 to 15 inches apart. If you are planting a large number of strawberries, plant them in rows to make it easier to control weeds. They should be in well-drained soil in full sun. Remove the weeds regularly with a hoe. You might also want to place a net over the berries to stop birds and squirrels from eating the fruit. Keep the strawberries watered to prevent the roots from drying out.

Place loose, clean, weed-free straw on the rows to prevent weeds and keep the fruit from lying on the ground. This will also help keep the roots of the strawberry

GROWN NEAR AUGUSTA, WIS.

WHI IMAGE ID 44511

Tall Tale Postcards

Do you think these strawberries are as big as a rail car? Why would someone send a postcard like this? People love to keep in touch. In the past, mailing postcards was a common way to send a message to a friend or family member. Some photographers were creative with their pictures. The image often told a story or myth by exaggerating information. Folks sent these fun postcards to portray their area as abundant in fruits and vegetables.

The Rural Free Delivery, or RFD, began in 1896 to deliver mail directly to farm families. Prior to this delivery system, families had to go into town to pick up their mail or hire a private service to bring out the mail. Many people sent postcards as get-well messages, for birthdays, holidays, and just to say hello. Have you ever sent a postcard to a friend?

roots cool, which is important to maintaining healthy plants. Straw is an ideal insulator, as it allows good air flow and protects the roots from the direct sun.

Strawberry plants send out runners, or new stems that grow from the roots of the parent plant. The runners eventually develop their own roots, resulting in a new plant. If you have a new strawberry patch, for the first 2 years, cut off these runners where they emerge. This helps the rest of the plant concentrate on growing strong roots and making fruit. After 3 years, you can allow the runners to make new strawberry plants. When runners appear, gently place them where you want more strawberry plants to fill in. If you are getting too many plants, cut out the runners you don't want.

New leaves and flower clusters form in the crown, or base of the plant, in early spring. The more crowns you have, the more fruit you will have. Strawberries turn red and ripen from the tip toward the leafy stem. They are ripe when they are completely red. Harvest them daily as you see the red color developing.

As winter approaches, the strawberry plant watches for temperature signals to harden off, or prepare for winter. After 2 or 3 frosts have hardened off the plants, cover them with 4 to 6 inches of weed-free straw, loose mulch, or garden fabric covering. The snow is an excellent insulator and is good protection for your plants. In the spring, when growth begins again, rake the straw away, but leave some at the base of the plants to act as the summer mulch.

OBSERVE, THINK, WONDER: Here is a photograph of brother and sister Cole and Cora Farwell holding strawberries they picked from a large strawberry patch. The photo was taken in June of 2020. How do you think the kids feel about picking strawberries? How are their facial expressions similar to or different from the couple in the photo at the beginning of this chapter? What is special about growing, picking, and eating fresh fruit? Why is it important to know where food comes from?

Cole and Cora Farwell with fresh-picked strawberries

Berry Snacks

Berry Smoothie

    1 cup mixed fresh berries (such as
          strawberries, raspberries, or blueberries)

    1 ripe banana

    1 cup vanilla or plain yogurt

    1 cup milk

Put the berries, banana, yogurt, and milk in a blender. Put on the lid. Blend the ingredients until they are smooth. Pour the mixture into cups. Eat right away. You could fill up cups and set them in the freezer for a while to enjoy as a "slushier" treat.

Berry Snack Crackers

    Strawberries, bananas, blueberries, or
          another fruit of your choice

    Strawberry cream cheese or a flavor of
          your choice

    Graham crackers

Wash the fruit. Carefully slice the fruit into bite size pieces. Spread cream cheese onto half of a graham cracker. Arrange the fruit on the cracker.

Chapter 8
GARDEN HARVEST

OBSERVE: Describe what you see in this photograph. What do you notice first? What is the setting of this photograph? Is this an image from the past? How can you tell?

THINK: What attitude toward food does this person have? Who is the audience this image was created for? What career do you think this person has?

WONDER: What do you think the person chopping vegetables is making? What other steps might someone take to prepare food from the garden for eating? What are some different ways to preserve food to eat later?

Harvested produce, including purple carrots, from the Apps family garden

Carson Gulley, pictured on the previous page, was born in Arkansas and made his way to Wisconsin to work as a chef in the summer at a lodge in Tomahawk. A visitor to the lodge was impressed with his cooking and invited him to work in Madison. In 1926, Carson Gulley began working as a chef at the University of Wisconsin–Madison. At the university, he developed a course for cooks in the US Navy during World War II. In 1949, he published a cookbook called *Seasoning Secrets: Herbs and Spices*. It was later revised and published as *Seasoning Secrets and Favorite Recipes of Carson Gulley*. In 1953, Carson and his wife, Beatrice, began hosting a popular cooking show, sharing their love of good food with a wider audience.

Like many chefs, Carson Gulley often cooked with fresh produce and herbs. A lot had to happen before those delicious foods made it into his kitchen, though. How do fruits and vegetables go from the garden to your plate?

HARVEST TIME

It is exciting to harvest produce from seeds you've planted and cared for. Keep these things in mind to be sure the experience is a safe and healthy one:

Zucchini squash flowers

- Wash your hands or wear garden gloves.

- Find clean, food-safe containers to collect your vegetables and fruits.

- Do not keep vegetables with signs of decay or rot. Instead, add them to your compost pile.

- Wipe off excess dirt from your produce with a clean towel.

- Store your produce correctly. For example, store berries unwashed. Wash them just before you eat them. Potatoes and tomatoes do not need refrigeration and should be stored in a clean, dry, cool place.

- Rinse produce under clean running water just before eating. Scrub firm produce such as carrots, melons, radishes, and potatoes.

WHEN TO HARVEST

Here are some tips for knowing when to harvest some common backyard garden vegetables:

Beets: This vegetable is ready for harvest when you see the color of the beet coming up and showing at the soil line.

Purple and green beans

Broccoli: You'll be eating the unopened flower buds of the broccoli. Harvest the broccoli before the flower heads bloom a bright yellow color. They probably won't look as big as the broccoli heads you see in the grocery store. After the first harvest, smaller side shoots should continue to form for later harvest.

Bush or pole beans: To find out whether it's time to harvest beans, go ahead and pick one. See if it snaps easily in half. Keep checking every day. Beans grow from tender to tough quickly if you don't pick them promptly.

Cabbage: Pick your cabbage when it feels solid. If you don't pick it, it continues to grow and splits open.

Carrots: Knowing when to pull up your carrots can be tricky. The tops of the carrot start to show at the soil line and you'll know how wide the carrot is. It is best to pull some out of the ground and see if they seem big enough to eat! It doesn't hurt the carrots to leave them in the ground a bit longer. Your garden carrots won't look like baby carrots from the store. Garden carrots grow in all shapes and sizes.

Corn: About 3 weeks after the corn silks form on each cob, they turn brown and look dry. Peel back the husks from a cob of corn while it is still on the stalk. Do the kernels fill out the cob? Test an ear of corn by poking a kernel with your fingernail. A milky looking substance comes out when the corn is ready to harvest. It's best to harvest corn in the morning, when the cobs are cooler. Keep freshly picked sweet corn in the refrigerator.

Cucumbers: Cucumbers grow quickly! Check the vines daily and harvest them when they are smaller, about 4 to 5 inches long. They should be green and smooth. Sometimes, they grow a bit oddly shaped, and that's okay! They still taste delicious! Some varieties of cucumbers feel prickly when you pick them. Just wear gloves when you harvest. These little spines wash right off.

Gourds: When the stem attached to the fruit begins to turn brown and dry up, it's time to harvest your gourds. Carefully twist them off the vine or cut the gourds from the vines with a scissors. Leave a bit of the stem attached and use them in your fall decorating.

Leafy greens, kale, and collard greens: Harvest leaf lettuce when the plant has reached about 4 to 5 inches in height. Use kitchen scissors to cut the outer leaves and allow the inner leaves to keep growing for harvest later. Kale is ready to pick when the leaves are about the size of your hand. Cut the outside leaves and not the center bud; this helps the plant continue to grow. Harvest collard greens when the younger leaves are about 10 inches long and dark green. Wash, dry, and chill your harvested greens.

Melon: The white spot on the bottom of a watermelon turns from white to a deep yellow color when the melon is ripe. When you carefully lift the melon and it breaks off the stem easily, it is ready to be picked.

A melon growing in a school garden

Peas: The best way to tell if peas are ready to harvest is to pick one and taste it! The pods should be ready to harvest about 3 weeks after the flowers appear. Pick snap peas when they are young and eat them whole, either raw or cooked. Harvest snow peas just as you begin to see the peas forming in the pod. Shelling peas, the kind of peas that need to be removed from their pods before they can be eaten, are ready when the pods swell and are a cylinder shape.

Peppers: Harvest peppers when they are the size and color you want. Peppers start out green and change color as they ripen. When they are ripe, it should be easy to pick them off of the plant.

Potatoes: Don't worry when you see the potato plants start to dry up and turn brown. This doesn't mean there is something wrong with your

Thai peppers growing in a container garden

Which of these tomatoes do you think are ready to pick?

potatoes! It means it's time to harvest. Carefully dig at the outer edge of a hill of potatoes. Gently shake up the soil to loosen the potatoes from the plant. Gather up the potatoes after letting them dry for a time on top of the soil in the garden. Wipe the dirt off of the potatoes, but do not wash them until you are ready to cook them. Store them in a cool, dry place without exposure to sunlight.

Pumpkins: A pumpkin will keep growing until you harvest it, as long as the vine and leaves are healthy. When your pumpkin has turned the color it is supposed to be and the vines are starting to dry up, it's time to pick your pumpkin. Keep checking the weather and be sure to pick your pumpkin before a hard frost is expected.

Radishes: In the spring, harvest radishes when you see the tops push up through the soil. They will be about one inch in diameter. Wash and store in the refrigerator. You can also wash and eat the radish greens.

Tomatoes: Tomatoes are ready to pick when they come off the vine easily. They will be fully red and a little soft to the touch. Some people like to pick tomatoes when they are almost ripe and let them sit inside to ripen up. This helps to protect your tomatoes from critters, such as squirrels. It also prevents them from falling off the vine, landing in the soil, and getting spoiled. Store ripe tomatoes in the refrigerator.

Zucchini and other kinds of squash: Squash grow extremely fast. Keep checking your plants. Harvest zucchini as they become the size you want. If you forget to check, they can become very large in just a few days!

SEASONALITY

Vegetables generally taste best when they are freshly picked. Have you heard the phrase about eating fruits and vegetables "in season"? Seasonality means knowing when fruits and vegetables are at their peak harvesting time. For example, in Wisconsin some strawberries begin to ripen in June. That's when you can buy locally grown strawberries that are in season.

Factors such as the climate where you live and the length of the growing season can make eating only fresh vegetables almost impossible for some months of the year. In colder months, fresh fruits and vegetables are shipped to grocery stores from warmer locations. This helps people to eat fresh food all year. But it's also good to be aware of what is in season where you live. For example, you might eat more strawberries in early summer and more apples in the fall! How much of the food that you eat is in season?

PRESERVING PRODUCE

How did people access fresh produce before there were large supermarkets? They preserved and stored foods to eat throughout the colder months. People have been preserving food for thousands of years. They found ways to keep food from spoiling and naturally decomposing. Many gardeners still use these methods so they can enjoy their garden produce all year long.

Preserving food prevents the growth of bacteria and other microbes. These tiny organisms make food taste bad and can make you sick. What are some ways to preserve and enjoy your garden harvest? Learn about and try these methods with produce from your garden. It's important to know the correct methods to ensure food quality and safety.

DRYING FOOD

Dried foods are lightweight to carry as a snack and are delicious. Some seeds of plants, such as sunflower seeds, dry naturally as part of their plant life cycle. Drying or dehydrating food is a method of food preservation. It takes the moisture out so that mold and bacteria cannot grow. To dry foods, you need the right amount of heat and low humidity. Warm air helps the moisture in the food to evaporate. If the air in your home is too humid, moisture from the food will not move into the air. The food you are going to dry should be just ready to eat, not overripe or under ripe.

You can air-dry some foods, such as peppers. With adult help, string the peppers together through the stems. Hang the peppers to dry in an area with good airflow. Many herbs can also be air-dried. Choose good, healthy stems of dill, basil, mint, or rosemary. Wash and dry the stems. Then, tie them together in bunches with string or twine. Hang the bundle to dry in a well-ventilated room for about 2 to 3 weeks. Remove the leaves from the stems when they are dry and store them for use in your cooking.

A store-purchased dehydrator uses electricity to provide warmth and a fan to provide air circulation. Using a dehydrator speeds up the drying time compared to air drying. You can also use it to dry a wider variety of foods. Follow the directions to safely dry produce. Apples, tomatoes, and sweet peppers are good first choices to try with a dehydrator. Store dehydrated food in a sealed container to keep out moisture.

Peppers drying at a farmers market

PICKLING

People all over the world use this method of preserving food. Pickling not only preserves fresh food but also changes the taste and texture in interesting ways. Traditional pickles are made with cucumbers, but other foods can also be pickled. Many people like to pickle asparagus, zucchini, or even watermelon rinds.

There are 2 pickling methods. One method makes a quick pickle by preserving the cucumber or other vegetable in vinegar. A second method soaks the cucumbers in a mixture of canning salt and other ingredients to keep them from spoiling. Canning salt (also called *pickling salt*) is pure granulated salt that doesn't contain iodine. It is different from regular table salt.

WORLD'S FAIR EDITION
1933 — CHICAGO — 1934

MODERN METHODS of HOME CANNING by Kerr

BULLETIN No. 834

Kerr is a company that makes jars used in canning. This Kerr canning booklet from the 1933–1934 World's Fair in Chicago helped people understand new canning techniques.

When you pickle something, you add acid to the vegetables so they can be safely canned with a boiling water bath. If you do not use the boiling water canning method, keep the pickles in the refrigerator. Be sure to carefully follow recipe directions for safe preservation when pickling. An adult should help with the boiling water canning process.

CANNING

Canning produce is a process of preserving food by using a boiling water bath or pressure canning. Many vegetables can be canned, including beans, corn, carrots, peppers, potatoes, and squash. Some people enjoy canning their garden produce, to make things such as tomato soup or juice, salsa, or jam. Since both methods require high temperatures, adult supervision is necessary. Still, canning can be a fun family or group activity.

It is important to select ripe vegetables without any insect spots or rot. The water bath method involves using the correct kind of jars and sealing lids. The food is set in the jars leaving adequate headroom, and then the jars are heated at the correct temperature for a certain amount of time. The heat from the boiling water bath drives out any air from the jar, sterilizing the food. The tight seal of the jar keeps out oxygen and prevents the growth of bacteria, mold, or yeasts. The pressure-canning method requires a pressure canner. (Not a pressure cooker!) In this method, the pressurized steam heat reaches high temperatures to seal the jars. For both methods, the completed jars are stored in a cool, dry place.

There are many resources and cookbooks that explain canning processes. Follow the directions and recipes to be sure your vegetables are correctly sealed and safe to eat.

FREEZING

Before modern refrigerators and freezers were common, many families dried or canned vegetables to preserve them. Today, if you have a freezer, you can preserve your harvest there. This is the simplest way to preserve all kinds of produce. Beans, broccoli, carrots, corn, peas, tomatoes, and zucchini are vegetables that freeze well. Use ripe and clean vegetables. Try to freeze the vegetables as quickly as possible after harvesting them. Trim and wash vegetables under cold water. Peel them if necessary. Cut into bite-sized pieces or choose to leave them whole. For example, if you are planning on using diced carrots later in a winter soup, freeze fresh carrots in smaller pieces.

Before freezing, many vegetables need to be blanched to stop any further ripening and help get rid of any dirt or bacteria. Blanching is a process in which you boil or steam vegetables briefly until they are partially cooked. This also helps the vegetables keep their nutrients and bright color. Vegetables such as broccoli and string beans need to be blanched before freezing. To blanch vegetables, bring a large pot of clean water to a boil. (Ask an adult for help with the stove and be careful when working with boiling water.) A good measure is to use one gallon of water for each pound of vegetables. Add the vegetables to the water. When the water returns to a boil, cook them for about 2 minutes. Carefully remove the vegetables from the water using a slotted spoon. Immediately plunge the vegetables into a bowl of ice water until they are completely cooled. When they are cool, drain them well in a colander.

Prepare airtight containers or plastic freezer bags by writing the date on the package. Freezer bags are specifically designed to keep out moisture. Fill the containers close to the top, but leave a bit of space because the food will expand as it freezes. If you are using a freezer bag, squeeze out any extra air before sealing it shut. The bags can be stacked flat to save space. Store frozen vegetables for up to 18 months. Frozen vegetables are best in cooked recipes, such as soups, stews, and casseroles.

Safe freezer containers of homemade salsa cool off until they are ready for lids.

Carson and Beatrice Gulley host their television cooking show.

Tomatoes do not need to be blanched before freezing. Just rinse, clean them off, and place them in freezer bags. To use the frozen tomatoes, remove them from the freezer a few at a time. To peel, just run the tomato under warm water. The skin slips off easily. Then, the tomatoes are ready to use it in your favorite recipe!

You can also freeze fresh fruit. Rinse the fruit and pat it dry. Fill up a freezer bag and remove as much air as possible. For soft fruits, such as strawberries and raspberries, set them on a pan in the freezer first to harden up. Then, transfer them to a freezer bag. Store frozen fruit for up to a year. Use frozen fruit in smoothies and icy desserts. Thaw it out to use in a pie, a crumble, or other baked dessert.

Herbs such as basil, chives, cilantro, dill, mint, and parsley can also be frozen to use later. Blanching them first helps keep their fresh flavor. Drop the herbs into boiling water for several seconds, and then carefully move them to a bowl of ice water for several seconds. Dry the herbs with a paper towel. Put some wax paper on a baking sheet. Spread the herbs in a single layer on the baking sheet and freeze for about an hour. Transfer the herbs to freezer bags. They keep their fresh flavor for about 3 to 4 months.

OBSERVE, THINK, WONDER: Earlier in this chapter you learned about one of Madison's most famous chefs. Do you wonder if Carson Gulley chose to use fresh ingredients from gardens and farms in Wisconsin for his recipes? What plans are you making for using the fresh vegetables from your garden? What kind of food preservation would you like to learn more about?

Garden Refrigerator Pickles

The canning process can preserve pickles for many months without refrigeration, but it can be a lot of work. For quicker results, try this recipe for garden refrigerator pickles. The pickles won't be preserved, but they will last in a refrigerator for several weeks. And they taste great!

8 cups unpeeled small cucumbers

1 ½ tablespoons canning salt (not table salt)

2 white onions cut into rings

1 cup chopped celery

2 cups sugar

1 cup white vinegar

1 teaspoon celery seed

1 teaspoon mustard seed

Slice the cucumbers, place them in a large bowl, and sprinkle with the canning salt. Mix the cucumbers and salt together. Let stand for at least 30 minutes. Drain off the resulting liquid and rinse the cucumbers with fresh water. Put the cucumbers back into the bowl and cover with fresh water. Let them sit in the fresh water for an hour. After an hour, drain the cucumbers.

Put the cucumbers into a 3-quart container that has a cover. Add the onions and celery to this container. In a medium saucepan, combine the sugar, vinegar, celery seed, and mustard seed. Heat over medium heat, stirring until the sugar dissolves.

Carefully, with adult help, pour this hot mixture over the cucumbers in the container. A funnel will help the liquid go into a jar without spilling. Let it cool and then put on the cover. Store the container in the refrigerator.

GARDEN PROJECTS

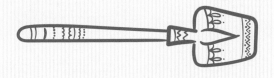

Chapter 9
THEME GARDENS

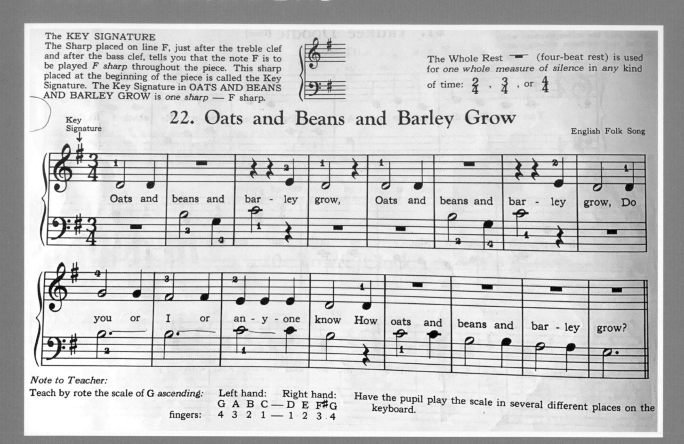

The KEY SIGNATURE

The Sharp placed on line F, just after the treble clef and after the bass clef, tells you that the note F is to be played *F sharp* throughout the piece. This sharp placed at the beginning of the piece is called the Key Signature. The Key Signature in OATS AND BEANS AND BARLEY GROW is *one sharp* — F sharp.

The Whole Rest ▬ (four-beat rest) is used for *one whole measure of silence* in any kind of time: $\frac{2}{4}$, $\frac{3}{4}$, or $\frac{4}{4}$

Key Signature

22. Oats and Beans and Barley Grow

English Folk Song

Oats and beans and bar - ley grow, Oats and beans and bar - ley grow, Do

you or I or an - y - one know How oats and beans and bar - ley grow?

Note to Teacher:
Teach by rote the scale of G ascending:

	Left hand:	Right hand:
	G A B C —	D E F♯ G
fingers:	4 3 2 1 —	1 2 3 4

Have the pupil play the scale in several different places on the keyboard.

OBSERVE: This is a different kind of primary source. It is a piece of music from a children's piano lesson book. What do you notice about this image?

THINK: Why do you think someone wrote a song about growing oats, beans, and barley? Who do you picture singing or enjoying this song? What do you think about when you read lyrics to a song?

WONDER: Are you wondering about the answer to the question the lyrics are asking? Do you wonder about the life of the person who wrote this song? What connections does this song have to gardening?

There are as many kinds of gardens as there are people who create them. What will your garden be like? Thinking about what you like to eat is a good place to start. You might also look to your daily life for ideas to design a special kind of garden. A song, a book, a movie, or a piece of art might provide inspiration. You may want to plan your garden around a favorite color, animal, or outdoor activity. Visit other gardens, an art museum, or a natural area to gather ideas of what you like. You might decide to draw or plan your garden first. The best thing about gardening is that you can change it every year. It's fun to learn about and discover what works and what needs to be improved for the next time. Would you like to try a theme garden project?

Here are some ideas to get you started:

What theme garden would you like to plant?

My Favorite Toys Garden: Choose plants that look like a jungle. Very large squash leaves might make a fun dinosaur habitat. Do you like small metal cars? Plan a space and build a little highway out of cardboard for your cars. Do you like trolls or other small characters? They can visit your garden too! Some people like to create a fairy garden where small elves and gnomes can visit. Create a gnome village out of recycled materials in a corner of your garden.

Reading Garden: Pick a favorite book with a garden theme. Try to recreate something from it in your garden. Another idea is to choose and grow plants that start with the letters in your first or last name. Make signs to spell out your name near these plants. Plan a space for relaxing with others near the garden. You can enjoy reading a book with a friend. Do plants grow better if you read to them? Try it and find out!

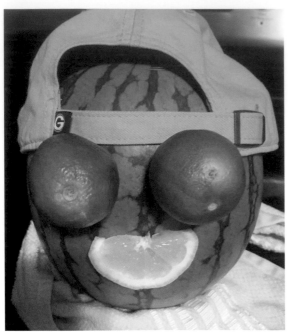
We made this watermelon character for a fun picnic.

Big or Small: For a giant's garden, plant seeds that are labeled "giant" varieties. A giant sunflower may grow to be 10 to 20 feet tall! For a tiny garden, choose very small varieties. You might try mini pumpkins and gourds.

Labyrinth or Maze Garden: Plan a section of your garden that is arranged around a pathway. A labyrinth is a meandering path that leads to a center. Some people say that walking slowly on the pathway promotes relaxation. A maze is made with taller plants, such as corn. Some mazes are designed to be like a puzzle, with paths leading to dead ends or loops. The fun is finding your way through.

Character Garden: Plant unusual colors of pumpkins, melons, and gourds, or vegetables of different shapes and sizes. When you harvest, you can create some "characters" to show your friends. Use a melon or pumpkin as the head. Attach gourds and small fruits or vegetables for eyes and a mouth. Slice up some raw vegetables and plan a tasting party.

Recipe Garden: Plan an area of your garden for all of the ingredients to top a pizza, including tomatoes, basil, oregano, and peppers. Or grow all the ingredients to make your own delicious salsa. Include tomatoes, garlic, cilantro, onions, and different kinds of peppers.

Rainbow Garden: Can you eat a rainbow? Use plants that show off each color of the rainbow: red, orange, yellow, green, blue, and purple. The colors might be part of the leaves, flowers, or vegetables.

Smell and Touch Garden: This garden has plants with many different smells and textures. Choose plants with soft leaves, such as lamb's ear, or herbs with wonderful aromas, such as rosemary, lemon verbena, and lavender.

Garden Salsa

You can grow most of the ingredients for salsa in a salsa garden!

2 large fresh garden tomatoes

1 garlic clove, crushed, or ½ teaspoon
    of jarred minced garlic

2 tablespoons of chopped onion

2 mild green chili peppers

8 sprigs of fresh cilantro

½ lime

¼ teaspoon salt

Tortilla chips, for serving

Dice the tomatoes and put into a bowl. Add the crushed or minced garlic to the tomatoes. Add the chopped onion. Mince the chili pepper, being careful not to touch your eyes. The oil on your hands from the pepper can sting. Wear gloves or be cautious. When you cut open the pepper, scrape away the seeds before dicing it. After you finish cutting, wash your hands. Add only a little chili pepper at a time. Taste it first to be sure it is not too spicy. You can always add more.

Take the leaves off of the cilantro stems. Chop up the cilantro. Add it to the salsa. Squeeze juice from the lime over the salsa. Sprinkle in the salt and stir. Serve with tortilla chips.

This salsa garden has everything needed for a batch of salsa.

Herb garden

HERB GARDEN

The best thing about growing your own herbs is using them in your favorite recipes! Some people like to grow herbs in containers on a deck or patio. You can also put herbs in the garden with your vegetables. Herbs like lots of sun, so plant them in a site that has all-day sun. Just like the soil for vegetables, you can test your herb garden soil to see if it is rich in nitrogen. Rake in compost to enrich the soil. If you notice that the soil has puddles of water after a hard rain, add more soil and build it up. Herbs like well-drained, moist soil for the first few weeks after planting. Then, let the soil dry a bit so the roots don't rot from too much watering.

You can start some herbs from seed and transplant them into your herb bed or buy small plants from a garden center. Plant them in the ground in rows or in groups, following the directions on the plant tag or seed package. Weed the herb garden as you would the rest of the garden. You may want to save the seed packages so you know what the herb leaves look like to compare to the weeds. When the herbs are about 6 inches tall, you can snip or pinch off leaves to use in recipes. When you do this, you are helping the plant grow and become bushier. Prune only the top leaves, so the leaves at the base can support and help the plant to continue growing.

Here are some herbs to try growing:

Basil: Basil is sensitive to the cold, so start growing it from seed indoors. Transplant the seedlings outside after the threat of frost has passed. Watch the early spring temperatures and cover your plants to protect them if the weather is predicted to be cold. Basil is great for making pesto for pasta and tastes delicious paired with tomatoes and mozzarella cheese.

Chives: This herb loves all-day sun and comes back year after year. Bees love to visit the purple flowers on chives. Chop up the green stems and add to scrambled eggs or use in a lettuce salad.

Cilantro: This herb grows best in cool, moist conditions. If the weather gets too hot, cilantro will bolt. That means it tries to flower and produce seeds as quickly as possible because it knows it can't survive hot weather. Pinching off the leaves frequently helps to keep it from bolting. You can also replant it once or twice in a season, if it dies. Cilantro tastes great in many salad recipes and is wonderful in homemade guacamole or salsa.

Mint: This herb grows well in pots. It spreads quickly and can take over space in a garden. When it is fully grown, harvest some leaves every day to keep it under control. A mint leaf looks wonderful in many desserts as a garnish. You can also use mint leaves to make tea. Bees enjoy the flowers on the mint plant.

Oregano: Water this herb only when its soil is dry to the touch. Oregano is great with pasta, soup, and meat.

Parsley: This herb does well in full sun or in a bit of shade. Be sure it has plenty of moisture. Chop it up and add it to salads or pasta.

Rosemary: This one is best grown from a small plant that you buy at a garden center. A container garden is a great place for rosemary. Snip some rosemary and sprinkle it on roasted meat or vegetables or add it to salads.

Sage: Buy sage plants rather than trying to grow them from seeds. Bees love this flower. It is great in pasta sauce and in your baked autumn squash.

Thyme: This herb is a perennial that returns each year. The woody stems grow low to the ground, so plant it where it has space to spread out. The pink or purple flowers are attractive to bees. Chop up the leaves and toss them into homemade salad dressing.

POLLINATOR GARDEN

When bees flit from flower to flower, they are doing an important job in your garden. Bees feed on and require both nectar and pollen. Nectar is the bee's main source of energy. Honey bees use nectar to make honey. The pollen provides protein and other nutrients. The bees use the pollen as larvae food. When a bee lands on a flower, pollen sticks to the tiny hairs on its body and legs. When the bee moves, it transfers the pollen from flower to flower. This process is called *pollination*. Pollination helps plants to produce seeds.

Flowers in your vegetable garden attract bees to come and visit. It is helpful to have flowers that bloom at different times throughout spring, summer, and fall. Bees are most attracted to flower blooms that are blue and purple. They are also attracted to flowers planted in clumps or patches.

Add flowering plants to your garden to attract pollinators.

Native flowers are plants that grow naturally in your area. They also attract bees. Bees will not go to plants that are unfamiliar to them. Native flowers are adapted to the climate in your region. Research your region's hardiness zone to determine the flowers that will grow successfully in your area. You could also ask for help from a University Extension office or a garden center.

Unfortunately, bee populations are declining. The reasons may be related to climate change, farming that involves only one kind of crop, or a change in land use. Some gardeners choose to avoid using chemical pesticides on insects in the garden. These chemicals might harm the bees as well. Research the best way to control pests using natural or organic methods in order to protect bees. You have a chance to welcome bees into your garden by making it a bee-friendly space. Plant flowers in your garden for the bees!

BUTTERFLY GARDEN

Butterflies are another important pollinator. They spread pollen between plants just like bees do. Many gardeners also like to attract butterflies for their beauty and color. It can be fun to watch them in each stage of their lives. An egg hatches to reveal a caterpillar, which then goes through metamorphosis to become a butterfly.

Near your vegetable garden, plant flowers to invite butterflies. A butterfly garden provides food and shelter through all stages of their life cycle. Plants and insects depend on each other. For example, the monarch butterfly depends on the milkweed plant. As the adult butterfly flies from flower to flower to drink nectar, it helps to pollinate the milkweed. The milkweed produces flowers and then seeds in a pod. The seeds produce more milkweed plants that grow and attract more monarchs. The monarch lays eggs on the underside of the leaves of the milkweed. After hatching, the larvae feed on the leaves without causing any damage to the plant.

For your butterfly garden, find a garden location that has 8 to 10 hours of sunlight a day. Check the hardiness zone for your area to determine which flowering plants grow well. Plants that are native to your area are best. Plant a variety of annuals and perennials that bloom at various times throughout the growing season. Butterflies are most active during the middle of the summer to late summer, so choose flowers that bloom then. Flowering bushes are a great addition to a butterfly garden because the leaves provide shelter.

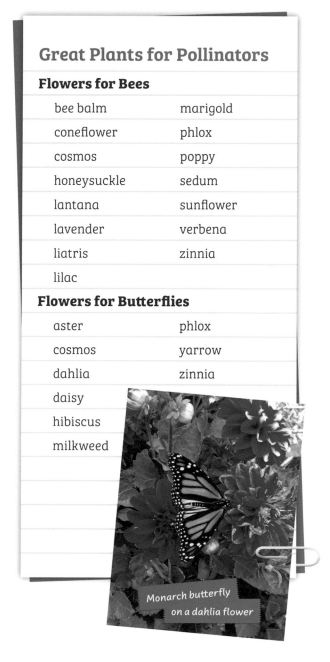

Great Plants for Pollinators

Flowers for Bees

bee balm	marigold
coneflower	phlox
cosmos	poppy
honeysuckle	sedum
lantana	sunflower
lavender	verbena
liatris	zinnia
lilac	

Flowers for Butterflies

aster	phlox
cosmos	yarrow
dahlia	zinnia
daisy	
hibiscus	
milkweed	

Monarch butterfly on a dahlia flower

Butterflies need water, but they can't drink out of deep, open water. Put one or two large rocks in your garden for butterflies; they will drink out of a water puddle on the rock.

HEALING GARDEN

Gardens help people feel better. Many hospitals plant an outside garden space. School gardens also often have space for gathering. Teachers can have class outside on a nice day!

You could set up a space in your own garden for relaxation. Consider adding some plants with various textures, shapes, colors, and smells to add a sense of peace in the space. Most people feel that stress goes away when they are outside in the fresh air. If you feel anxious or have a problem to solve, spending time in your garden can be helpful.

OBSERVE, THINK, WONDER: Why would someone write a song about planting oats, beans, and barley? The page of music at the beginning of this chapter is from a children's piano lesson book from 1950. It's a version of an old English folk song from the 1800s. Folk songs often tell us something about the daily life of the people who once sang them. Who do you imagine sang this one? Folk songs are passed down through generations. They are often sung by schoolchildren or appear in children's music books. Do you wonder if the student who practiced the piano with this song also had a vegetable garden? What things might inspire you to design your own theme garden?

Zucchini Recipes

At harvest time, I always seem to have too many zucchini! Here are 2 favorite ways to prepare it.

Watch your zucchini carefully because it grows quickly! You can still eat it when it's large. Just cut out the seeds first.

Zucchini Noodles

Zucchini noodles, also called zoodles, are really easy to make. Wash your zucchini but leave the skin or outer layer on. Use a vegetable peeler to create long strips, or noodles. Stir fry them in a pan with olive oil, onions, and a tablespoon of minced garlic. Or, stir fry them in sesame oil and soy sauce. Don't overcook them. The noodles should be cooked until they are just tender, like pasta. They will look a little wilted but still have a crunch. Top the noodles with parmesan or your favorite cheese and diced fresh tomatoes.

Award-Winning Zucchini Bread

I won a blue ribbon at the Dane County Fair with this bread when I was involved in my 4-H cooking project. It is definitely a family favorite!

3 eggs	3 cups flour
2 cups sugar	1 teaspoon baking soda
2 cups peeled and grated zucchini	1 teaspoon salt
1 cup cooking oil	1 teaspoon cinnamon
2 teaspoons vanilla	½ teaspoon baking powder

Preheat the oven to 325 degrees. Coat 2 large loaf pans or 4 smaller loaf pans with butter or shortening and then dust with flour.

In a large bowl, beat the eggs. Then add the sugar, grated zucchini, oil, and vanilla. Mix together until smooth. The mixture will look lumpy because of the zucchini. In another bowl, stir together the flour, baking soda, salt, cinnamon, and baking powder. Add the flour mixture to the zucchini mixture a little at a time. Mix well each time until thoroughly blended.

Carefully spoon the mixture into the bread pans. Bake the 2 large pans for about one hour (or bake 4 smaller pans for 45 minutes). You will know the zucchini bread is ready when a toothpick inserted in the middle comes out clean. Cool the pans on a rack for 10 minutes before taking the loaves out. Enjoy! This bread also freezes well.

Chapter 10
GARDEN ACTIVITIES

ROUND LAKE SCENE, WILD ROSE, WIS.

POST CARD

Dear brother How
are you havent
heard from you
for a long time
we are all fine saw
all the folks last
night up town all
are O. K. it is hot and
dry we need rain.
aful bad it is so
dry. answan Minnie.

CORRESPONDENCE HERE

NAME AND ADDRESS HERE

Mr. Herman apps.
Ashton
South Dakota
%o Sam Nevill.

U.S. POSTAGE
1 CENT

OBSERVE: This is a postcard from a sister to a brother. What do you notice first? How is the layout of a postcard different from a letter? How much did a postcard stamp cost when this was written? What does the picture on the front show?

THINK: This is a postcard from about 1918. What do you learn about this time period from this primary source? What tool did the writer use? How do people communicate today? What would be the same? What is different?

WONDER: Do you wonder why it was important for Minnie to write about the weather to her brother? Why is keeping track of the weather important?

This postcard was written to my grandfather, Herman Apps, from his sister Minnie. When Herman was 18 years old, he left his family farm in Wisconsin to work in South Dakota. He had a temporary, seasonal job harvesting wheat. The address on the card is directed to Herman Apps in Ashton, South Dakota. However, the card is written "in care of" Sam Nevill. Mr. Nevill was Herman's boss. Here is what the postcard says, with punctuation added for clarity:

> Dear brother, How are you? Haven't heard from you in a long time. We are all fine. Saw all the folks last night up town. All are O.K. It is hot and dry. We need rain offul [awful] bad. It is so dry. AW [answer] soon. Minnie

Minnie felt it was important to write to her brother about the weather on her postcard. She lived in a rural area. Her parents were farmers. Having a successful growing season depended fully on the weather and the amount of rain during a summer. In 1918 it was important for farmers to observe and keep track of the weather. It's still important today, not just for farmers but for anyone who has a garden.

Minnie's postcard represents one way that people communicated with each other in the early 1900s. Have you ever written to someone about your garden? In what ways do you share your love for gardening? This chapter has ideas for activities related to gardening. Some will help you to become a better gardener, and some will help you share what is going on in your garden with others. Some are just for fun! You'll find that your garden is a great place to find inspiration for all kinds of projects.

Ben Horman used his journal to record what birds, animals, and insects he saw near the garden.

Another student used a journal to record what they learned about insects found in the garden.

JOURNALING

Keeping a garden journal is one way to look back on your progress as a gardener. You'll look closely at your garden and record those observations to help you notice what changes over time. Nobody else has to see it, unless you want to share it. You can use any kind of notebook to write in. Your journal is a useful written record of details you might forget, such as frost dates, when and where you planted seeds, what pests bothered your garden, and what solutions worked or didn't work. You can draw a map of your garden or sketch illustrations of your growing plants. Try to write or draw in your journal at least every week. Write down whatever seems important to you.

Another activity for your journal is to keep track of weather observations. What is the weather like each day: sunny, cloudy, partly cloudy, rainy? It is important for a garden to get enough rain so that your vegetables will grow. You can use your observations to decide if your garden is getting enough rain, or if you'll need to water it. For each day, record the high temperature, low temperature, and amount of precipitation. If you have a rain gauge near your garden, record the amount of water it collects. You may also want to keep track of other factors in the weather that may affect your garden, such as amount of wind.

It's also fun to write about how you experience a garden. Try writing about how you feel, what you are learning, what mistakes you make, and how you solved a problem. Writing about things is a way to reflect and think. Did you see any birds near your garden? What did you hear while you were in the garden? Did you smell anything?

How to Make a Rain Gauge

You can make your own rain gauge with supplies from around the house. You'll need a clear one-liter soda bottle, some small rocks, a permanent marker, a ruler, and scissors for this activity.

1. Cut the top off of a clear one-liter soda bottle.
2. Place some small rocks in the bottom to allow the bottle to stand upright.
3. With a permanent marker, mark the level of the top of the rocks inside as 0, about 2 inches up from the bottom.
4. Measure and mark inches and half inches from your 0 point.
5. Fill the container with water up to the 0 mark.
6. Place the top part of the bottle upside down into the container. It will act as a funnel and collect water.
7. Place your rain gauge on a flat surface outside.
8. Wait for the next rain and record the rainfall amounts.

A rain gauge is useful for tracking rainfall in your garden.

Here are some writing prompts to help you get started:

- My favorite plant is . . .
- The seeds that are doing well are the . . .
- The seeds that seem to be struggling are . . .
- When I am in the garden I feel . . .
- My favorite place in my garden is the . . .
- My least favorite thing about the garden is . . .
- Something I noticed about the creatures living near/in my garden is . . .
- Things I need to do in my garden this week . . .
- My list of my harvest for the year . . .

Date: _____

Temperature: _____°F _____C°

Weather: _____
(Sunny, cloudy, partly cloudy, etc.)

Observations: _____

_____

_____

_____

_____

_____

Today I saw _____

_____

Today I heard _____

_____

Today I touched _____

_____

Today I smelled _____

_____

An example of how a garden observer could set up a notebook page to make garden observations

Some gardeners also like to keep a gratitude journal. Every day after recording information about the garden, they write down something they are grateful for. It is a way to remember that gardening brings joy to those who tend the plants and eat the food. Gardeners feel a connection to the seeds and soil. They are grateful for the opportunity to care for the garden that feeds them.

MATH ACTIVITIES

There are many ways to make math connections in a garden. When you plan your garden, figure out a budget. A budget is a document that lists the money you spend and money you earn. How much will it cost to buy materials to make a raised bed or to buy seed packets? Will you do any chores for your family to earn money to spend on seeds and supplies? Use graph paper to draw a map of your garden to scale. Figure out how to show where the rows are on the graph paper. Keep track of the height of plants with a ruler. As they grow, switch to a yardstick. Count the number of tomatoes on a plant, and after they ripen, weigh them.

As your ability with carpentry tools improves, investigate and research how to build a trellis or a small fence. Construction projects involve adding, subtracting, multiplying, and dividing with fractions. Sometimes you need to know how to calculate area, volume, length, and width. These math concepts will help you figure out a plan, follow directions, and build your creation.

Discover connections with geometry in your garden. Look for symmetry in insects or in plants. Bilateral symmetry means an object has a left side and a right side that are mirror images of each other, like a butterfly. In radial symmetry, the same pattern repeats around a point in the middle. Flowers such as aster and daisy show radial symmetry. Their identical petals surround a center. Do you see any symmetry in your garden?

Did you know there are many fractals in nature? A fractal is any pattern that when cut into parts is like a smaller version of the original picture. Basically, a fractal is a repeating pattern. The seeds in the head of a sunflower plant form a fractal pattern. An unfurling fern demonstrates spiral patterns. What other patterns do you observe naturally in nature?

SCAVENGER HUNT

A garden scavenger hunt, by yourself or with some friends, is a great way to practice observing your garden. Use a magnifying glass to look closely at stems, leaves, and flowers. You may see interesting insects, rocks, worms, and birds. Make a list of things to search for in your garden. Adding categories such as "things to hear" or "things to smell" is also fun. Make a list for each game player. Who can find all of the things on your scavenger hunt list? You can ask them to check things off the list or take photos of their scavenger hunt finds. Gardens change constantly, so you can play as many times as you want. Record what you find each time, and compare the results to the next time you invite friends to visit your garden.

Here are some ideas of things to search for:

- An ant or other insect
- A squirrel
- A small bird
- A pink (or any color) flower
- Rough or soft leaves
- A plant taller than you
- A vine with a flower
- A vine that feels rough
- An unripe vegetable
- A vegetable that is growing under or above the ground

ARTS AND CRAFTS

Many books, blogs, and websites are devoted to garden arts and crafts projects. You'll discover many ways to incorporate art into a garden. As you watch your plants growing, what art projects are you inspired to make?

A favorite activity is to use duct tape to make a bracelet decorated with garden-related items. Duct tape is a long-lasting adhesive tape, also called cloth tape. It is very strong and water resistant. Cut a piece of duct tape long enough to fit around your wrist. With the sticky side out, wrap the tape around your wrist and tape it to itself. Then find beautiful petals, leaves, tiny rocks, pieces of grass, or anything you think is interesting. Attach them to your bracelet until you fill up all the sticky parts. Have fun arranging the things in a beautiful and interesting design.

Two students show the duct tape garden bracelets they made at school.

Garden Art Ideas

- Paint on scrap wood or safe upcycled materials to make row labels or signs for your garden.

- Think of a name for your garden and make a sign for the entryway.

- With adult permission, make a colorful mural near your garden. A garden mural is a painting on a wall or the side of a building. It's fun to work on a mural with friends!

- Find interesting items for your garden plants to grow on. An old ladder, bicycle wheel, window frame, or interesting wire design can make an excellent trellis.

- Design an artistic fence with long sticks, twigs, bendable branches, and twine.

- Create and paint tiny houses out of recycled materials for garden gnomes to visit.

- Make flower crowns to wear.

- Use upcycled and recycled materials to create a sculpture for your garden.

- Use dry garden materials, such as daylily stalks or cornstalks, for weaving. Weave yarn or other natural materials through the stalks to make colorful designs. It will be like weaving on a giant garden loom!

(Continued on next page)

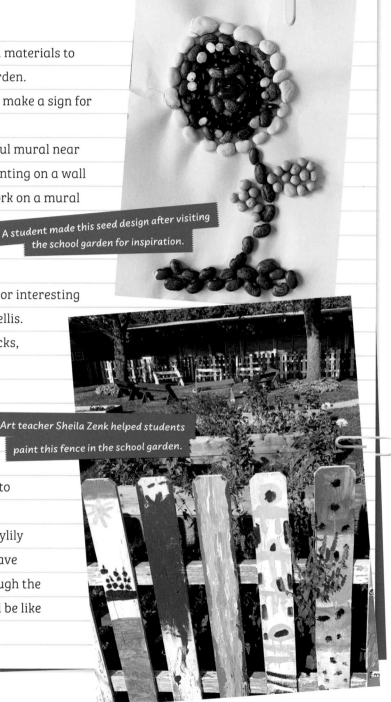

A student made this seed design after visiting the school garden for inspiration.

Art teacher Sheila Zenk helped students paint this fence in the school garden.

Garden Art Ideas (continued)

- Create a space in or near your garden to paint, sing, or write and perform a play.
- Reuse plastic bottles. Carefully cut them in strips starting at the neck of the bottle and fold the strips down to create "flowers." Decorate your garden with these plastic flowers.
- Use natural materials to create a giant nest as a space to sit in and read a book.
- Design jewelry with dandelions or other flowers and stems.
- Press flowers in newspaper or between the pages of a large book. Create art with these dried flowers.
- Make a seed picture. Use glue (not a glue stick) to arrange dried seeds into an interesting design.
- Find special rocks. Paint faces or messages on them. Cut out felt shapes and glue them onto the rocks to make garden creatures.
- Build a birdhouse or bird feeder to welcome birds into your garden.
- Make leaf or bark rubbings.

This creature decorates a school garden.

GARDEN ORAL HISTORY PROJECT

Oral history is a method of learning about past events from the spoken stories of people who lived through them. It is a way for you to engage with history as you collect information and learn how to be a historian. You can interview someone about the past or ask someone to talk about their feelings about life today compared to life in the past. It's their story that you are interested in. What can you learn?

As you work in your garden, think about others who gardened in the past. Why did people garden? Was the garden their main source of food? Did they garden to share food with others? Do they have any advice for gardeners today?

Find someone you can interview. That person could be a relative, neighbor, or friend who is older than you are. Think of questions that you'd like to ask this person. Is there a central question you'd like to ask or a topic you would like to know more about? Are you interested in a certain time period? What did they grow or eat in that time period? What recipes do they remember? How did they cook the food they grew? Did they preserve food to eat later? Write down a few of your questions. Perhaps you can use your garden journal for this activity.

Invite your interview subject to visit your garden and take a tour. Explain what you are growing and why you chose the plants in your garden. Then find a comfortable, shady spot to sit and relax with your garden guest. Ask your questions and be a good listener. Record their answers by writing them down or recording them digitally. You may think of new questions as you listen. Remember to consider this person's perspective. How does the person's background influence the story? Do you have anything in common with this person? How is your garden experience the same as or different from what you are hearing? An oral history interview is a great way to get another person's perspective and to learn about history.

OBSERVE, THINK, WONDER:

This is a photo of my grandfather, Herman Apps, and his friend Sid Simon, in 1918. Herman is 18 years old in this photograph. This is about the time he was away from home working in South Dakota, helping with the wheat harvest described at the beginning of this chapter. I wonder what his life was like. I wonder if he enjoyed the adventure of going to a new place, living on a different farm, and helping with the harvest. Herman returned to Wisconsin and raised his family on a farm. The family always had a kitchen garden near the farmhouse. Every year, Herman planted a vegetable garden, even when he moved off of his family farm and into town. He looked forward to planting his garden in the spring. What do you know or wonder about your ancestors' lives? Saving primary source documents from your own family is a great way to observe, think, and wonder about your family story.

Herman Apps and Sid Simon when they were working in South Dakota, in 1918, when Herman was 18 years old. The postcard from the beginning of the chapter was sent to Herman at the time of this photo.

Paul's BELTCH
(Bacon, Egg, Lettuce, Tomato, and Cheese) Sandwich

My husband, Paul Bodilly, says he just kept adding his favorite things to his bacon, lettuce, and tomato (BLT) sandwich until he realized that it spelled out BELTCH. Can you make a sandwich with ingredients that spell a word? Here's the recipe for Paul's sandwich:

bacon

egg

lettuce

tomato slices

cheddar cheese

2 slices of wheat bread

mayonnaise

Fry the bacon in a pan until just crisp. Take the bacon out of the pan. Set it on paper towels to absorb the grease and to cool. In the same pan, fry one egg. Toast 2 slices of wheat bread. Spread some mayonnaise on the bread. Build your sandwich with the bacon, egg, lettuce, tomato slice, and cheddar cheese.

FINDING YOUR ROOTS

Chapter 11
EARLY GARDENERS

OBSERVE: What do you notice about this tool? What does it look like it's made from? How old do you think it looks?

THINK: Who do you think used this tool? What did they use it for? How is it similar or different from tools gardeners use today?

WONDER: Who were the first gardeners in our state? What do you wonder about Wisconsin's first gardeners?

The story of land in our state must begin with the Native populations. Various groups lived here for hundreds, even thousands, of years before European settlers arrived. How do we know about people from so long ago? Many of these groups have their own records of their past. They may have passed down information from one generation to the next through oral storytelling traditions. Historians also look for physical evidence. Archeologists carefully dig and find clues about the past. Artifacts, such as stone tools and pieces of pottery, help researchers ask and answer questions about the past.

From these sources, historians have learned about the way these early groups lived. As Wisconsin's land and climate changed over thousands of years, people who lived here adapted to find sources of food. About 1,000 years ago, some Native peoples started to garden. The ability to grow their own food changed their lives in important ways. When we learn about these changes, we can think in new ways about our own gardens. How do the foods they grew compare to what people grow now? Did they use similar tools or methods? In what ways did being able to grow their own food affect people's lives?

PALEO-INDIANS AND ARCHAIC INDIANS: 10,000–800 BCE

Wisconsin's earliest people are called Paleo-Indians. From around 10,000 BCE, they lived as hunters and gatherers. During this time, the climate was too cold for planting and gardening. Fewer edible plants were able to grow in the colder temperatures, so people had to travel far and wide to gather berries and nuts. Small family groups traveled on foot to hunt mammals such as deer, elk, mammoths, and mastodons. Archeologists found spear points used for hunting from this time.

You might recognize this era as the time when large animals such as the mammoth and mastodon roamed the state. Visit the skeleton of a large mastodon skeleton at the Geology Museum on the University of Wisconsin–Madison campus. The skeleton was found near Boaz.

As the climate in Wisconsin grew warmer, about 9,000 years ago, new kinds of trees, such as oak and maple, started to grow. More small mammals could be found. With more food sources, the people of this time, who archeologists call *Archaic Indians*, began to stay in one place for short periods of time. Like the Paleo-Indians, they traveled with the seasons to find food and resources. When it was cold, they used a rock overhang or built shelters to keep warm. When it was warmer, they gathered berries, nuts, seeds, and edible plants. They harvested wild rice in the fall. They hunted deer and caught fish. During this time, people most likely did not plant gardens as we think of them today.

WISCONSIN'S EARLIEST GARDENERS: 800 BCE–1630 AD

Over time, the ways Native people lived changed. From about 800 BCE until 1630 CE, Native people continued to spend time hunting and gathering food from the forests and wetlands. But some groups started staying in one place for longer periods. They lived together and built shelters with wood frames covered in animal hides, bark, and woven mats. This meant they could start growing some food. They began planting and harvesting corn and squash. They also were the first group in Wisconsin to begin making pottery containers for cooking and storing food. Archaeologists later named people from this era *Woodland Indians*.

Woodland Indians are also well known for the effigy mounds they built. Some of the mounds are shaped like animals or other shapes with special meaning. The practice of mound building is one sign that people had started to form communities and stay in one place for a longer time. The land that includes effigy mounds remains sacred. For this reason, people are not allowed to dig, walk on, or destroy remaining mounds.

WHI IMAGE ID 78519

This effigy mound outlined in chalk at Lake Koshkonong is shaped like a bear.

A sign at Picnic Point in Madison reminds visitors to be respectful of effigy mounds there.

A Three Sisters garden, with corn, squash, and beans growing together

Around 1000 CE, a new group moved north along the Mississippi River to what is now Wisconsin. Archeologists call this group of Native people the Mississippians. The Mississippians built a well-organized community surrounded by high walls. This was the village of Aztalan, which is now Aztalan State Park. Because they stayed at the same place all year, the Mississippians grew and stored crops, such as corn and squash, to eat during the long winter. Researchers are not sure what happened to this group of people or why they seemed to disappear.

Archeologists named another group of people the Oneota. From about 1000 CE, the Oneota lived in farming villages near rivers or lakes. At least some of the Oneota stayed in these villages year-round. In 1989, researchers found pottery near La Crosse. The site is part of 3 villages called the Tremaine Complex. They also uncovered Oneota longhouses, storage pits, fire hearths, and stone tools.

While the Woodland Indians began to grow some crops, the Oneota were skilled farmers. Oneota farmers grew corn, beans, and squash. These vegetables grow well together and became known as the Three Sisters. The 3 types of plants grew in a mound together and provided well-balanced nutrition. The Oneota probably also fished, hunted animals in the woods, and gathered wild rice in the wetlands.

As these early groups grew more of their own food, you can see the ways in which their lives changed. They had a bigger variety and more stable food sources. They moved around less and built more permanent housing. They were able to form larger communities.

FIRST NATIONS

Early peoples such as the Woodland and Oneota were the ancestors of many of the First Nations who live here today. According to historian Patty Loew, the Menominee, the Ho-Chunk, the Ojibwe, and the Forest County Potawatomi were here when European explorers first came to what would later be called Wisconsin in the 1600s. The Brothertown, Oneida, and the Mohican Indians migrated here in the 1820s.

When European settlers arrived, they wanted land and other resources. The US government forced Native peoples to move and relocate. Land was ceded to the United States by Native nations through treaties. Because of cultural differences, Native peoples believed they were signing an agreement for mutual access to the land, not that they were giving up all rights to the land. Some Native groups fought against relocation, while others were forced to leave but found their way back. The Ho-Chunk, Ojibwe, and Menominee peoples lost large amounts of land in this way. Several groups, including the Sauk, the Meskwaki (also known as Fox), the Sioux, some of the Potawatomi, the Kickapoo, and the Nebraska Winnebago, were driven from Wisconsin entirely.

Between 1887 and 1934, Native children were taken from their homes and placed in day schools or boarding schools. The purpose was for children to give up their own language and customs. They were taught other ways of agriculture. The reality is Native people had been growing food successfully for a very long time.

WHI IMAGE ID 33806

This painting is an artist's idea of an Oneota farmer with his village in the background.

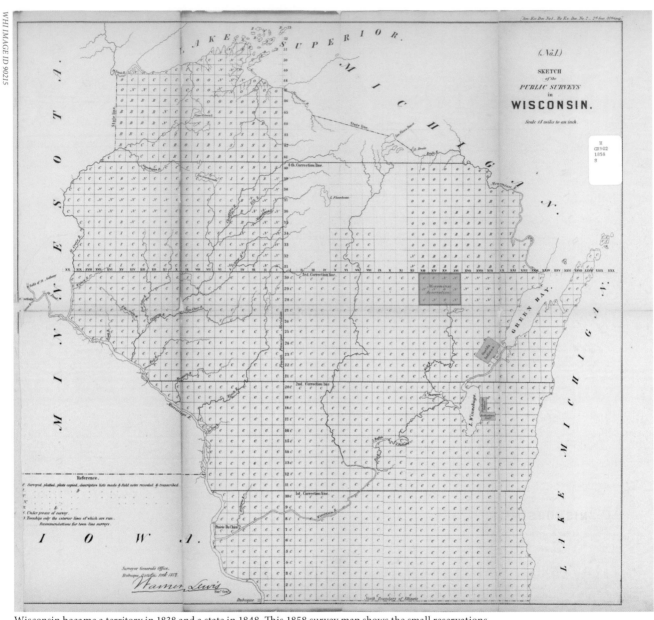

Wisconsin became a territory in 1838 and a state in 1848. This 1858 survey map shows the small reservations (highlighted) where the Oneida, Menominee, Stockbridge, and Brothertown nations had to live.

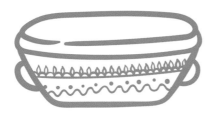

Despite the loss of their lands and their treatment by non-Native settlers, Wisconsin's Native peoples have found ways to keep their gardening traditions alive. One example can be found at Olbrich Botanical Gardens, in Madison, which added an indigenous herb garden in 2021. The garden includes Ho-Chunk corn and squash, Arikara yellow beans, Potawatomi lima beans, Cherokee trail-of-tears beans, and Oneida tobacco.

The project was led by Rita Peters, an Olbrich staff member with connections to the Menominee and Ho-Chunk. Peters described the importance of reviving Native gardening traditions to *Madison, WI Patch*, a community newspaper:

> No longer having access to our traditional foods changed our relationship with our food and the natural land. Our seeds are our relatives that we've spent time with over generations, cultivating and working together to feed our communities. This relationship between seeds and people plays an important role in supporting indigenous cultures, economies, communities and values.

OBSERVE, THINK, WONDER: The photos at the beginning of this chapter shows a clamshell that would have been attached to a bone or wooden handle. This was a gardening tool used by the Mississippians to cultivate crops at Aztalan. Although little is known about the people who lived in this community, archeologists have uncovered various tools and pieces of pottery. What do you think can be learned from these artifacts? What do you still wonder about the lives of the Mississippians of Aztalan?

The Three Sisters

Do you know why corn, beans, and squash are called the Three Sisters? The reason is these 3 plants help one another when they are planted together in a mound. The Three Sisters continue to be important to First Nations agriculture.

The Three Sisters are considered the sustainers of life. Together, they provide many nutrients needed to keep someone healthy and active. First Nations storytellers have several myths about how the Three Sisters came to be. In one Oneida story, the "Sky Woman" was falling to earth from the sky. On the way, she grabbed all the seeds necessary to provide life on earth.

In a Three Sisters Garden, the stalks of corn serve as poles to support the bean plants as they climb. In return, the beans help the corn. Beans convert nitrogen from the air into forms that can be absorbed by plant roots, fertilizing the soil. Squash is planted at the base of the corn and beans. The squash leaves are large and prickly. They help keep away pests, such as raccoons. The leaves also provide shade to keep the soil moist and prevent weeds. These 3 plants are companions in the garden, helping one another to grow.

Steps for Planting a Three Sisters Mound

1. Make a mound of dirt and plant 3 corn seeds in the center of the mound, about 6 inches apart. Allow the corn to begin growing.

2. When the corn is about 4–6 inches high, plant 4 pole bean seeds halfway down the sides of the mound. Plant them in the corners of the mound, in the 4 directions to match north, south, east, and west. Train the bean vines to climb up around the corn.

3. After the beans have emerged, plant 2 squash plants at the outside of the mound as a border. As the squash grows, wrap the squash vines around the edge of the mound. The squash leaves should help keep the ground moist and prevent weeds from growing near the corn and beans.

4. If you are planting more than one Three Sisters mound, plant each mound about 3 feet apart.

Summer Salad with Corn, Beans, and Squash

This recipe is inspired by the Three Sisters garden and uses corn, beans, and squash for a summer salad. An adult can help with the cutting, especially with cutting the kernels off of the fresh sweet corn.

½ cup olive oil, divided

¼ cup white vinegar

2 teaspoons salt, divided

dash of pepper

1 15-ounce can of butter beans, rinsed

4 medium size tomatoes cut up

1 medium zucchini, cut into ½-inch chunks

4 ears of fresh sweet corn, kernels cut off
of the cob

1 minced garlic clove

Whisk together ¼ cup of the oil, vinegar, 1 ½ teaspoons of salt, and pepper in a bowl to make a dressing. Add the beans, tomatoes, and zucchini and toss to coat the vegetables with the dressing.

Harvested sweet corn from the Apps family garden

Heat the remaining ¼ cup of olive oil over medium high heat in a pan on the stove top. Add the corn kernels and remaining salt and cook until just beginning to turn brown, about 6 minutes. Add the garlic and cook about 30 more seconds. Add the corn mixture to the bean mixture.

Cover the salad and let it sit for at least 30 minutes to allow the flavors to blend.

Chapter 12
SETTLING AND PLANTING

OBSERVE: Take a look at this photograph of Julius Koehler and his garden. He and another man are holding a very large cabbage and a root vegetable. What else do you notice?

THINK: What are you wondering about this photograph? Maybe you're wondering how they grew such large vegetables, or how they made the vegetables appear so large. If you guessed that this photograph was changed to make the vegetables look larger, you're right! Even in the early 1900s, photographers changed pictures for a purpose. This one was a promotional card to encourage people to move to northern Wisconsin and start growing a garden.

WONDER: Was having a garden important in the early days of our state? How does learning about the history of gardening help us find our roots?

The sign at the Olson family farm in Vernon County, Wisconsin

In this Olson family photo, Ruth is the youngest girl in the front.

Gullick Oleson Dybing was born in the county of Rogaland, Norway, in 1828. When he immigrated to the United States in 1854, he left from the seaside city of Stavanger. He dropped the name Dybing, changed the spelling of his middle name, and became Gullick Olson. In 1856, he purchased 40 acres of land in Vernon County, Wisconsin. After serving in the Civil War, he returned and added more land next to the land he already owned. After he died in a farm accident at the age of 47, the farm was taken over by his son Gabriel. Gabriel married a neighbor, Sophia Sebion, in 1889. They had 8 children. Their oldest son, Clarence, died of pneumonia in France at the end of World War I. He was buried in France. The Olson farm was given to their second oldest son, Otto. He married a Swedish woman, Ella Lundgren, who he met in college in St. Paul, Minnesota. They married on October 17, 1918. Ella wrote, "The war was under way, so no time for an extended honeymoon. We traveled back to WI in a model T Ford Touring car. How well I remember this trip. No paved roads or Hwy signs." Otto brought his new wife home to the Buena Vista Farm, which Otto had purchased from his father. On the farm, they raised purebred registered Jersey cows and white Leghorn chickens. Otto and Ella had 5 children, the youngest named Ruth.

Growing up in the 1940s, Ruth Olson fondly recalled that her mother was always outside in the kitchen garden. Ruth remembered, "My mother loved being outside in the summer more than any other place on the farm. She grew all the usual things in the garden: tomatoes, lettuce, cucumbers, peas, beets, carrots, radishes. When it came time to harvest peas, Ella ate them right out of the garden. To pick them, she would hold up the 2 bottom corners of the apron she was wearing and carry the peas into the kitchen. Her kitchen apron often became handy as a 'basket' for harvesting. We canned so many vegetables for the winter. She learned how to do it from her mother, and then she taught me." Ruth and her family participated in many 4-H food and home activities. She won many ribbons at the fair with her projects.

Today, this farm remains in the Olson family as it has for 160 years. The family continues to have gardens as they did many years ago when the first "Olson" arrived in Wisconsin. Ruth Olson's story is part of my garden history because she is my mother. This story of a Norwegian family gardening in Wisconsin is part of my garden history story.

Many families have stories similar to this one. People came to Wisconsin in the past for different reasons. Some came to work in the fur trade, mines, or logging camps. Some were looking for a new start, a better life, or a piece of land to call their own. Whatever brought them here, an important part of making a new home was feeding themselves and their families. Settlers planted kitchen gardens or larger crops. Some brought seeds, tools, skills, or gardening traditions with them. Then they learned what grew well in Wisconsin's climate and soil. Many of these early gardeners passed down their knowledge and traditions through generations.

Ella Olson's Fresh Rhubarb Cake

Ruth Olson remembers rhubarb plants that grew near some large boulders close to the kitchen garden on her farm. As a child, she helped cut the stalks to use for this spring recipe.

½ cup butter

1 cup brown sugar

1 cup buttermilk

1 egg

1 teaspoon vanilla

2 cups flour

1 teaspoon baking soda

¼ teaspoon salt

1½ cups fresh rhubarb cut
    in ¼-inch pieces

For the topping:

½ cup white sugar

1 teaspoon cinnamon

Preheat the oven to 350 degrees. In a large bowl, cream the butter and 1 cup of the sugar. Add the buttermilk, egg and vanilla.

In a separate bowl, mix the flour, baking soda and salt. Add the cut pieces of rhubarb to the flour mixture to coat the rhubarb. Add the flour mixture to the sugar mixture and mix well.

Pour the mixture into a greased 9x13 pan. Combine the ½ cup of sugar with 1 teaspoon of cinnamon. Sprinkle the cinnamon sugar on the top of the cake batter. Bake in the oven for 35 to 40 minutes.

Fresh-picked rhubarb

Six cooks stand ready to serve a meal in a logging camp dining room.

SETTLING IN WISCONSIN

Wisconsin's earliest non-Native settlers were fur traders, followed by miners and loggers. As author Jerry Apps writes in *Wisconsin Agriculture*, "In each of these eras, the settlers had to survive and feed their families, and they did so with vegetable gardens and small-scale farming." At first these groups did not spend much time building permanent homes. They did not stay in one place long enough to grow their own food. Early miners sometimes lived in holes dug into a hillside. This earned them the nickname "badgers." Later mining towns were established on lands of the Kickapoo, Sauk, Meskwaki (Fox), and Ho-Chunk Nations. Miners started gardening to provide food for their families or became part-time farmers. In addition to hunting and fishing, they now had fresh vegetables to eat. By 1860, the former lead mining region in southwestern Wisconsin had been taken over by agriculture.

In the northern part of the state, logging camps were established to cut down acres of pine forests. Many logging camps were most active in the winter. Some men were farmers during the growing season and left home to work at a logging camp during the winter. The camp cook was responsible for feeding the crew. Do you imagine he used food from the previous summer? He could feed lots of men with stored potatoes, onions, and root vegetables. After loggers cut down trees, the lumber was processed at lumber mills. Some logging and lumber companies planted company gardens, and a few operated farms. The companies used the produce they raised to feed their workers. Communities sprang up around the lumber mills as the workers and their families built homes, and some of them planted gardens for food as well.

Matthew and Julia Stephenson and their son William Clinton pose with vegetables from the Menomonee River Boom Company garden near Marinette in 1895. Employees of the lumber company and their families could grow food there.

For most settlers, growing food for their families was an important part of living and surviving in their new country. Early gardeners planted seeds; weeded and watered throughout the growing season; and harvested crops in the fall. They dried plants such as herbs and onions. They made cabbage into sauerkraut in crocks. They also grew plants for dying cloth, herbs used in medicine, and flowers to remind them of home. Because Wisconsin winters are cold, settlers needed to prepare for survival in the winter months. In root cellars, they stored vegetables such as carrots, potatoes, beets, parsnips, rutabagas, and turnips. The cellar was also the place to store shelves full of jars of pickles made from cucumbers or watermelon rind, as well as canned meat and vegetables. Settlers used a canning process similar to what families do today, to preserve food in airtight, sealed jars. They could enjoy this food throughout the long winters. Then, in the spring, imagine their joy as they prepared their garden plots for the summer's vegetable seeds!

As the land was cleared of forests, land agents invited more people to settle in Wisconsin. They advertised the state's rich soil, access to water sources, and good climate for growing. The photo at the beginning of the chapter shows how an image could be used to encourage families to move to the north to settle and start a new life there. The US government also wanted more people to settle in places like Wisconsin. In 1862, Congress passed the Homestead Act. The word *homestead* means a house, especially a farmhouse, and the other outbuildings that make up a farm, such as a barn, chicken house, or hog pen. The law gave land to settlers who met certain requirements. A homesteader had up to 5 years to clear the land, build a house, and live there. Part of the agreement was that they had to plant crops and grow food on their land.

GROWING DIVERSITY

Black Americans also came to live in Wisconsin in the 1700s and 1800s. Like Native peoples and European settlers, they too faced the challenges of feeding their families in a new place. Some were enslaved by early settlers and later freed.

A group portrait includes members of the families who lived in the Pleasant Ridge community around 1895.

Thomas Greene, long-time resident of Pleasant Ridge, pictured around 1920

Others migrated from the South, escaping slavery or seeking a better life after the Civil War. Near present-day Beetown in Grant County, a community of African American farmers was called Pleasant Ridge. In 1848, a former enslaved man named Charles Shepard moved to Wisconsin with William Horner, who purchased more than 1,000 acres of farmland in Grant County. Charles and Caroline Shepard, along with their 3 children, Harriet, John, and Mary, went to work for Horner. So did Charles's brother Isaac and Isaac's future wife, Sarah Brown. In only a few years, the Shepard brothers saved enough wages to purchase 200 acres of their own land. They called their hillside community Pleasant Ridge. Soon, the Shepards were joined by others escaping enslavement. All of these homesteaders most likely grew vegetables to feed their families.

For the residents of Pleasant Ridge, the farming community meant the start of a new life and the ability to provide for their families. Although Charles Shepard died fighting in the Civil War, Isaac became one of the area's most prosperous farmers. Many other residents of Pleasant Ridge also enjoyed success growing crops. German, Irish, and English farmers joined the Black residents. The population grew to about 100 residents, who farmed a total of 700 acres of land.

Similar communities took root in other areas of the state. In Vernon County, about a dozen Black families from the South settled in Cheyenne Valley. The people of Cheyenne Valley grew corn, oats, wheat, barley, and rye and also raised pigs and dairy cows. Neighbors shared tools and helped one another with planting and harvesting. Although most residents of Cheyenne Valley arrived with very little, they succeeded in their new home by working the land.

Throughout the 1900s, people were drawn to Wisconsin because of its rich resources or the many opportunities to find work here. Others found a home here when mistreatment forced them to leave their home countries. Since the 1940s, Wisconsin has had large numbers of new arrivals from Latin America and Asia, along with smaller numbers from southeastern Europe and later Africa. Many Black Americans also migrated to Wisconsin from the Southern United States during that time.

Following World War II, Wisconsin farms were growing more vegetables than ever before but didn't have enough people to work in the fields. The state's farmers recruited Mexicans and Mexican Americans living in the US Southwest to fill those jobs. Many of them were Tejanos, Texans of Mexican descent. These farm workers worked hundreds of thousands of acres of farmland in Wisconsin, growing peas, sweet corn, cucumbers, cherries, snap peas, lima beans, red and sugar beets, and tomatoes. Thousands harvested cherries in Door County. These farm workers filled an important need but were often not treated well, with low pay and poor living conditions.

Many migrant farm workers stayed for the growing season but returned to their homes in Mexico or the US Southwest after each harvest. Others put down roots in Wisconsin. Some found better-paying jobs in cities, where they planted small kitchen gardens to help feed their families. Some found more permanent jobs in agriculture. In the book *Mexicans in Wisconsin*, author Sergio González describes the experience of Arturo Landeros, who was born in Texas. For many years, he managed a group of migrant workers who worked in bean and potato fields. Then the family purchased a 160-acre farm of their own in Rusk County,

This painting shows Mexican farm workers harvesting cucumbers in Wautoma in the 1960s. It was painted by Seferina Contreras Klinger and shows her grandmother, Aurelia M. Contreras, and her uncle, Fidel Contreras.

Wisconsin, in 1957. When the Landeros family arrived on their farm, they were the only Spanish speakers in the entire county. As more Mexican Americans settled in Wisconsin communities, they brought their language, their culture, and their foods. They opened restaurants and grocery stores and started selling produce at farmers markets.

How do you think the arrival of a new group affects a community? Can you think of any foods or recipes you like that were brought here from other places?

TRANSPLANTING TRADITIONS

Leaving almost everything behind did not mean that people did not bring things with them. Wisconsin's diverse settlers brought their history, traditions, and ways of living to a new place. This meant bringing seeds, food knowledge, and recipes along to their new home. Many immigrants continued to grow foods and cook recipes from their homeland. For example, German immigrants grew cabbage to make sauerkraut. Norwegians grew potatoes to make lefse, a soft flatbread. Mexican Americans grew hot peppers and tomatillos, which look like small green tomatoes. Hmong Americans who settled in Wisconsin began planting the Thai eggplant and bitter melon they enjoyed growing and eating back home.

A great way to discover more about your community's food and gardening traditions is by visiting your local farmers market. At a farmers market, you can buy vegetables, fruits, and herbs directly from the person who grew them. Many small-scale farms and even some gardeners sell their produce at farmers markets. Walk around and see if you can spot anything unfamiliar. Feel free to ask questions to find out where it came from and how to grow it! You might discover a new fruit or vegetable. And you might hear some interesting stories about how different foods came to be grown in Wisconsin.

What's your family's garden story? Did anyone in your family have a garden before you? Do you know what they planted and why? How were their reasons for gardening similar or different from your own? If you're not sure, you might try the oral history activity in chapter 10 to find out more. As you learn about your own family history and that of the different groups who settled in Wisconsin, think about the phrase "putting down roots." People say this when they are talking about making a permanent home someplace. Maybe they are thinking of how a plant's roots grow into the ground to help it thrive in that spot. How does planting a garden help someone feel connected to a new place?

It's interesting to think about gardening as part of the definition of "being settled" in an earlier time. To own land as part of the Homestead Act, a person was required to plant and harvest crops. The time period was not just for one growing season, but for 5 years. That was how they proved to the government they planned to stay on the land.

What do you think it means to "be settled"? Were earlier fur traders and miners settled in Wisconsin in the same way as the other homesteaders? Think about the amount of planning, patience, and work it takes to plant a garden and how that affects your connection to a place. There is something special about putting seeds in soil. Growing a garden was an important part of being settled in a new community.

Old World Wisconsin

At Old World Wisconsin, an open-air museum in Eagle, Wisconsin, visitors can tour farms and gardens for a glimpse of how Wisconsin's early settlers lived. They learn about the machinery settlers used and the crops they grew. Author Marcia C. Carmichael, author of *Putting Down Roots*, describes the gardens at Old World: "Re-created, historically accurate gardens complement the settings of a dozen homes from various ethnic backgrounds and delight the senses of visitors." She also writes about the traditions settlers brought with them, "The immigrants found comfort in growing familiar plants and added favorites when they could. Precious seeds and plant material brought from the Old Country quickly went into the ground and received careful nurturing. Seeds or tubers of the best specimens were collected and saved for the next season's crop."

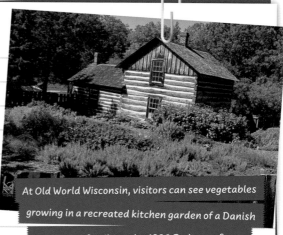

At Old World Wisconsin, visitors can see vegetables growing in a recreated kitchen garden of a Danish immigrant family at the 1890 Pedersen farm.

Conclusion
THOUGHTS FOR GARDENERS

OBSERVE, THINK, WONDER: Do you wonder about the children in this picture? This is an image from a scrapbook kept by the Neighborhood House in Madison, Wisconsin. In this photo from 1939, Edith, John, and Caroline Cordio are posing in front of some flowers at their house on West Washington Avenue, in Madison, Wisconsin. Do you imagine them helping with this garden? Did they plant seeds, pull out weeds, or enjoy the flowers?

139

The Verona Public Edible Garden let people pick their own vegetables in the summer of 2020.

Another free garden in Sugar River asked visitors to take "just enough" for themselves and leave the rest for others to enjoy.

In each chapter of this book, you practiced observing, thinking, and wondering about a primary source document related to gardening. How does learning about gardening in the past help you think about gardening today? What did you learn about your relationship to the food you grow and eat? What things are still missing for you? Where could you find answers to your questions?

If someone asks you what you like to do for fun, would you answer planting seeds, working in your garden, and cooking food that you've grown? Gardening is one way to connect with the world around you.

GARDEN AS A COMMUNITY

People who have the space and opportunity to garden are privileged to be able to do this. Not everyone has the time, space, and resources to have a garden. At times, people need help with obtaining their basic needs: a safe place to live, clean water to drink, and healthful food to eat. In some communities, access to affordable, good quality, healthful food is difficult. Community gardens are one way to help. Many schools, neighborhoods, and churches offer space for gardens. Do you have a garden like this where you live? Could you help with a community garden project?

In the spring of 2020, many people became unemployed because of closures due to the COVID-19. A group of gardeners in Verona, Wisconsin, worked to increase their community's access to high-quality fruits and vegetables. They built, planted, and maintained raised garden beds that were freely available to anyone who needed the produce. They hoped to bring the community together as they grew vegetables.

BE A GARDEN CHANGE MAKER

Can you think of ways to improve the lives of others with a garden? A community change maker listens and is willing to learn. They also dig in and do the work to improve the lives of others. Some of this important work can happen in a garden!

If you garden in a community space, invite people from different age groups and backgrounds to work together. The garden provides a common interest for everyone. A garden is a space for talking, listening, and learning from each other. Produce from the harvest can be given to local food pantries or sold at a market to raise money for a cause you feel is important. Planting flowers and creating new art to display in a garden are ways to promote change in your community.

OBSERVE NATURE CLOSELY

When you spend time caring for seeds in soil, you develop an appreciation for nature. In your journal, write your observations and feelings about the outside spaces around you. A special project is to study one particular tree or a small marked area. Return to it every day and look closely to observe any changes you notice. When you take the time to connect with nature, you begin to understand the importance of caring for your environment.

You may decide to do further research about climate change, soil, ways to save energy, or food systems. Plan an inquiry project to explore how nature and people are connected. Ask important questions. Don't rely on one source of information. Find evidence to support answers to your questions about people, communities, and your environment. Your garden provides for you, so find ways to go deeper and give something back.

BE CREATIVE WITH OTHER PEOPLE

It's fun to be outside with other people! Gardening is active, physical, and rewarding. Your reward is more than a bountiful harvest. Being in a garden helps your mood. It increases your social and emotional well-being. People seem to be happier after spending time in a garden.

Find a creative way to spend time outside. Create art; sing a song, write a poem, put on a play in a garden. Invite a friend or a neighbor. Leading by example creates a ripple effect! Think about how your garden can inspire your friends, family, and neighbors to make space for outdoor creativity. How does a garden inspire you?

Squash and corn plants at the Apps family garden in midsummer

FIND YOUR ROOTS

A garden is a good place to think about history. You have practiced observing, thinking, and wondering about the past in this book. History is about how you understand yourself in connection with the past and with the world today. Learning about garden history is a way to connect to the past while growing and eating delicious food today.

When thinking about history, remember that you are part of it. Think about this: Who is going to remember your story? You are the author of your own life story. What should someone in the future know about how you planted seeds in soil? What will people remember about you and what you were thinking? As you plant a garden, keep notes, create drawings, direct videos, or take photos to record your history. Part of your own story can begin in a garden, planting seeds in soil.

ACKNOWLEDGMENTS

This book would not be possible without the support of my husband, Paul Bodilly. Thanks also to our adult kids and grandkids, who bring us so much joy and continued adventures in nature.

Thank you to my dad, Jerry Apps, for his wisdom, in and out of the garden. My mom, Ruth Apps, taught me canning techniques, jelly making, and all things tasty and wonderful in the kitchen. Thank you to my brother Steve Apps, former staff photographer at the *Wisconsin State Journal*, for his professional help editing photos. Thank you to both Steve and Natasha Kassulke for their work in our family garden in central Wisconsin. Thanks to Jeff and Sandy Apps for their help with recipes and support with this project.

Thanks to See Yang, for your family recipe; Mai Zong Vue for sharing your refugee story; Sheila Zenk, art teacher and school garden creativity expert; Emily, Cole, and Cora Farwell for a fun strawberry day; and Wayne Horman, for soil science information.

Thanks to Kurt Griesemer, elementary education specialist for the Wisconsin Historical Society, for providing comments and feedback.

Thank you to the staff at the Wisconsin Historical Society Press, including Press Director Kate Thompson, Marketing Director Kristin Gilpatrick, and Erika Wittekind, Wisconsin Historical Society Press editor extraordinaire.

INDEX

This index points you to the pages where you can read about persons, places, and ideas. If you do not find the word you are looking for, try to think of another word that means about the same thing.

ABOUT THE AUTHOR

Susan Apps-Bodilly is the author of the children's book *One Room Schools: Stories from the Days of 1 Room, 1 Teacher, 8 Grades*, and coauthor with Jerry Apps of *Old Farm Country Cookbook*, both published by the Wisconsin Historical Society Press. She is a member of the Society of Children's Book Writers and Illustrators, the National Council for the Social Studies, and the National Science Teachers Association. Susan has been an elementary and middle school educator in rural and urban school districts in Wisconsin and Ohio. She currently teaches second grade and enjoys adventuring in nature in all seasons.